More Great Praise for Books by Don Silver

The High School Money Book

"The book has an amazing number of very practical bits of advice for high school students and anyone else who is overwhelmed by the number of personal financial decisions they make every day."
—Douglas Haskell, Director of Professional Development
 Economics Center for Education & Research
 University of Cincinnati

"Great job! A book like this has been a long time coming for high school students and their voyage into life, but this was well worth the wait."
—Paul Harney, Social Studies Educator, *Cazenovia High School*

"The *High School Money Book* is a must read for every student BEFORE they graduate—their parents should read it too!"
—Bill Uffelman, President and CEO, *Nevada Bankers Association*

"Don Silver did a great job of presenting those important concepts high school age kids need to know. I would recommend the *High School Money Book* not only to young adults, but also to anyone who needs a refresher on the basic skills and concepts needed to navigate the financial waters of one's life."
—John Meeks, President, *North Carolina JumpStart Coalition*

"Very comprehensive. The format is very practical and intuitive."
—Tameria L. Vickerson, Ph.D., Director of Programs
 Florida Council on Economic Education

"Contains 101 smart ways to handle finances."
—*School Library Journal*

"Don Silver's *High School Money Book* is a great place to start learning about money matters—even for those who haven't stepped into the halls of a high school for decades."
—Kara McGuire, who writes a Gen X and Y personal finance column and blogs for the *Minneapolis Star Tribune*

"Money is a favorite graduation gift for high school seniors. But how about giving a manual to go along with your cash gift? The *High School Money Book* by Don Silver would be an ideal gift."
—Bruce Brinkman, Certified Financial Planner/Business Columnist *Rockford Register Star*

"The subject matter in this easy-to-read book is so relevant to the personal finance, saving, budgeting and life preparation skills all kids need to learn before they leave high school."
—Rosanna Jacobsen, a VP with *Colonial Bank, N.A.* and President of the *Florida Jump$tart Coalition for Personal Financial Literacy, Inc.*

"The *High School Money Book* talks straight to teens about money. Teens learn that they can be happier and more self-sufficient if they master money matters now rather than correct money mistakes later. They learn how to make important decisions about working, shopping, using credit, preparing for college, making a budget, keeping financial records and making money grow by saving and investing."
—*Jump$tart Coalition for Personal Finance Literacy*

"A 'Money Smarts 101' for high school students...Enthusiastically recommended."
—*Midwest Book Review*

"The *High School Money Book* is an ideal way to open family dialogues about personal finance. This is a *must have* for every teen."
—Ronni Cohen, Executive Director
Delaware Financial Literacy Institute — Delaware Money School

"Don Silver has written the perfect roadmap, a must-read! Buy it today, read it, live it."
— Dr. Paul B. Farrell, columnist, *DowJones/MarketWatch.com* and author of *The Millionaire Code; The Winning Portfolio* and *The Lazy Person's Guide to Investing*

"A great resource for students and teachers."
— Ellen Potere, Business Education Educator, *Sayville High School*

"Simple yet well written…It keeps up with the times and bridges subjects that some parents may not be covering with their teens."
— Joyce Montgomery, President
  Oklahoma Jump$tart Coalition for Personal Financial Literacy

"A very well written book organized for quick reference and easy reading."
— Mike Sullivan, Director of Education, *Take Charge America*

"The *High School Money Book* should be required reading for all high school students. Don has a knack for introducing and explaining financial concepts in a simple, story-like manner that draws in the reader."
— Jim Walsh, Editor in Chief, *Forefield Inc.*

A Parent's Guide to Wills & Trusts

Jane Bryant Quinn put *A Parent's Guide to Wills & Trusts* on her holiday gift list in *Woman's Day*.

"Excellent book…What also differentiates this book…is the writing itself. It is clear. It is concise. It is clever."
— *Los Angeles Times*

"This book is different: it's concisely written, uses simple language and features an easy-to-understand format."
— *Chicago Sun-Times*

more

"A practical, easily understood book that should be read by grandparents and parents alike."
—*Grandparenting* (a *Universal Press Syndicate* column)

"*Must* reading for all parents. This isn't just another probate/estate book. Tips on avoiding family disputes, considering tax impact and dealing with special circumstances such as divorce, second marriages and special beneficiaries are remarkably specific and contain details no other general will book offers."
—*Wisconsin Bookwatch*

Baby Boomer Retirement

"Astute and provocative."
— *Los Angeles Times*

The Generation X Money Book

"This is an outstanding book...The book promises tips and it delivers."
—*USAToday.com*

Teach Your Computer To Dance:
Make Your Computer, Mobile Devices and the Internet Perform for You

"Great book for the computer genius or novice. It's a must-have book for people of all professions."
—Rochelle Stewart, *The Boston Herald*

"You can pick any page at random and find yourself saying, 'That's a good idea.'"
—Andrew Kantor, Technology Columnist, *USA TODAY*

High School Money Book

Don Silver

Adams-Hall Publishing
Los Angeles
www.adams-hall.com

Library of Congress Cataloging-in-Publication Data

Silver, Don
  High school money book / Don Silver.
     p. cm.
  Includes indexes.
  ISBN-13: 978-0-944708-74-3
  1. Teenagers--Finance, Personal. 2. High school students--Finance, Personal.
  3. Finance, Personal. I. Title.

  HG179.S4745 2006
  332.02400835--dc22

                        2006034443

Adams-Hall books are available at special, quantity discounts for bulk purchases, sales promotions, premiums, fund-raising or educational use. For details, contact Adams-Hall Publishing at **800.888.4452** or **info@adams-hall.com**.

Printed in the United States of America
10 9 8 7 6 5 4

Contents

Part Five
Money-Smart Ways to Give

Part Six
Money-Smart Ideas to Discuss with Your Parents

Part Seven
Money-Smart Ways to Prepare for College

Part Eight
Money-Smart Ways to Bank

Part Nine
Money-Smart Ways to Handle Paperwork

Part Ten
Money-Smart Ways to Make Your Money Grow

Part Eleven
Money-Smart Ways to Work

Part Eleven (continued)
Money-Smart Ways to Work

Part Twelve
Money-Smart Ideas for the Future

Appendix

Index

Introduction

There should be a class in high school called "Money Smarts 101" to teach you how to handle money. That's what this book is designed to do.

Knowledge about money matters provides a sound basis for making decisions about purchases, saving, investing, college and working.

Spend ten minutes a day reading this book and you'll get a quick education to help avoid some of the hard knocks of life.

Better to learn what to do than what you should've done.

What is money?

Although the form of money has changed over time, its main purpose has remained the same—to help people buy and sell products and services.

Probably your first thought about money is that it's only dollar bills and coins. Money is much more than that. It includes checks, credit cards, debit cards and ATM cards, too. To some people money also includes stocks, bonds, real estate and all other forms of investment.

And even as you're reading this page, the definition of money is changing. New Internet currencies and cyber forms of money are appearing all the time and many of these virtual forms of money can be turned into real money.

Throughout history, many different objects have been used as money including seashells, cattle, gold and silver.

Paper money first appeared 1,000 years ago in China. Until then, gold and silver were the favorite choices for money throughout much of the world.

Marco Polo wrote with some amazement how the Chinese actually accepted pieces of paper as money (it wasn't so amazing since the Chinese emperor threatened death to anyone who refused to accept this paper currency as money).

You'll be dealing with many different forms of money all of your life. You might as well start learning now about smart ways to handle money.

How to use this book

This book is divided into 12 parts and contains 101 smart ways to handle money. Although I recommend that you start at the beginning and read the book in order, the book is designed to allow you to jump to topics of interest by looking at the table of contents or the index. Every topic in the book will be of interest to you now or in the near future.

PART ONE
Money-Smart Ways to Think

1. The true value of money

To be smart in handling money, you first need to know money-smart ways to think about money.

Money is part of a two-way street. You trade or exchange money for products or services you want. When you hand over money to make a purchase, it's too easy to forget what you are really giving up.

In other words, you need to remember the value of money.

Money is earned through work requiring your time and your life energy. At your age you may have time and energy to spare, so should you care now how you spend them? The short answer and the long answer are both yes. As the years go by, decisions about how you spend your money will affect your schooling, the jobs you take, your relationships with others and the amount of stress and satisfaction in your life.

The problem with spending money too carelessly is that you can become trapped in a job, a career or a relationship that "requires" you to stay there to pay the bills.

Knowing in advance the true cost and value of lifestyle and purchasing decisions can allow you to have financial and personal freedom.

The key for you is to handle (and not too often mishandle) money in ways that are right for you. Understand the value of money and then use your money wisely.

2. The successes and mistakes of others

One of the most overlooked ways to become knowledgeable about money is to find out how money has affected people you know. Ask your parents, their friends and your relatives what they did right with money and what they would've done differently.

Don't "reinvent the wheel" when it comes to money. Use the successes and mistakes of others as a starting point.

You don't need to follow the advice of others. However, learn to be a great interviewer and a smart listener. We all learn best by asking questions, lots of them. And people love to talk about themselves.

Find out how they feel about their material possessions, debts, jobs and relationships.

As you talk to others, chances are you will see how a person's general personality may be similar to a person's pattern of financial actions and inaction.

If you ask the right questions, you'll get a self-taught financial education that's worth years of college.

3. The secret to being successful

All things considered, it's more fun being rich than poor. However, being successful in money matters is not the same as being successful in life. Having a lot of money or possessions may not even make you happy.

Plenty of very wealthy people always seem to want more than they have. If having more isn't always the path to success, consider an alternative. Happiness and success in money matters (and life) largely depend on whether you are grateful for what you do have.

We all want to have nice things and that's healthy. What's unhealthy is when you don't appreciate what you do have and are endlessly wanting what's new, what someone else has or what you can't afford to have. You may never satisfy your wants.

The key is to have balance in your life. Try to attain your personal and financial goals but make sure you're not paying too high a price in the quest, especially when it comes to financial goals.

Think about people who suffer through a disaster such as a hurricane or an earthquake and their home, their possessions and maybe their business are demolished. Are their lives over? No.

Listen to the words of survivors of disasters and you'll hear how "thankful" they are that they and their loved ones survived. It's at moments like these that people appreciate what they do have.

Do you want to be successful? Here's the secret. Do your best, appreciate what you have and you may be richer than anyone you know. Beware of the addiction to always want more.

4. Needs vs. wants—what you need to know

One key way to know more about money is to learn about yourself.

If you can separate your *needs* from your *wants*, you'll be far ahead in the money game and the game of life as well.

Here are a couple of examples.

You may need a car to get to college or to work. You may want a fancier car than you can really afford.

If you satisfy your wants, you may end up working extra hours and days at a job you really don't like to pay for a fancier car. This extra work may mean that you have less time and energy for the other parts of your life—including enjoying your car and being with friends.

A more expensive car may mean going into debt that will take years of work to pay off. By choosing a less expensive car, you may gain financial and personal freedom.

As the years go by, you'll have other material wants and purchasing decisions, such as deciding whether to buy a house or a condo. You may want to buy a more impressive home than what you need. The cost to you may be working many extra hours or staying in a job you hate just to pay the mortgage.

Four key questions

Here are four key questions to ask yourself so you can separate your needs from your wants:

1. Am I trying to impress anyone else by this purchase?

2. Am I making the purchase to feel better about myself?

3. How much will this purchase really cost me in time, effort, money and lost opportunities?

4. Am I satisfying a want or a need?

There is no one right answer for everyone. The choice is yours. Just make sure you're aware of the consequences before you satisfy your wants.

5. Time is money

What does managing your time have to do with money? Everything.

If you can't manage your time, you won't be able accomplish what is really important to you. Waste time and you'll have less time for school, your career, your relationships and your friends.

Manage your time wisely by knowing what's important to you. Sit down and make a three-column list with the three most important goals to you right now, five years from now and 10 years from now. Balance your personal, professional and financial goals.

Use this list as your guidepost to make day-to-day decisions about how to "spend" your time.

Once a year take a look to see how you're doing in meeting your goals. If you're really serious about improving your life, review and make a new list every six months.

If you're spending your time wisely, you'll be a richer person by having more time to do what is really important to you.

6. Resisting peer pressure

One of the greatest obstacles to financial and personal happiness is peer pressure. Boy, is it hard to resist.

If everyone else has certain clothes or the latest electronic gizmo, it's natural to want those same things, too.

You know what? You're going to face peer pressure the rest of your life. Now is the time to develop confidence in your own choices and life decisions.

Learn to deal with peer pressure now or you'll be a "sheep" all your life. There's the expression "Just say no." Instead, "Just say me." Ask yourself, "What's best for me?" Don't ask what everyone else is doing.

The price of giving in to peer pressure can be a loss of self-respect and self-esteem plus a mountain of debt.

Why do you think it's called peer "pressure?" It's pressure whether you give into it or you resist it. Be tough. Be strong. Be your own person.

7. The price of being "in" and tulip mania

You've seen or heard about many crazes where everyone starts buying the latest fashion or investing in the "in" thing. These crazes didn't start recently. A classic case that infected adults occurred nearly 400 years ago in Holland.

Amsterdam, the capital of Holland, had become a wealthy city in the 1600s. People started to exhibit their wealth by building larger houses. There wasn't much land available so gardens had to be small. The main feature of those gardens was tulips.

Somehow, everyone of every economic class had to have tulips — and not just any tulips, but the best tulips. Tulip bulb auctions started popping up (auctions didn't start on the Net). Many of the buyers at those auctions didn't want the tulips as flowers to enjoy — they wanted bulbs as a way to make money, big money. Bulbs were being resold for large profits and more people became involved as time went on.

You've probably heard of the Stock Market Crash of 1929 that brought on the Great Depression. But the first big market crash was the one in tulips that happened in 1637. Once people woke up and started to wonder why they had traded houses and other valuables for tulip bulbs, the price of tulips went down fast. Soon, many people had bulbs of little value but no money or houses.

Always remember tulip mania before you invest or go for the latest trend.

8. Voluntary simplicity and you

One way to improve your life (and your money situation) is to simplify how you live. The key to living more simply is to really think about (be more conscious of) purchasing and lifestyle decisions. Simplification can stretch your time and your money and reduce stress.

Usually, simplification leads to greater freedom in your life by reducing your dependence on having "things." You can gain freedom to make college, career and life decisions and changes without being shackled by a financial ball and chain.

Six steps to simplify your life

1. Before making any purchase, ask yourself how much of your life energy this purchase will cost.

Will you need to work 4 hours, 40 hours or 4,000 hours to pay for this purchase? This isn't a new thought. Over 200 years ago, Adam Smith wrote about the "labor theory of value." Smith felt that the value of any object could be measured by the amount of work for which it could be exchanged.

2. Will this purchase make your life easier, more satisfying or more worthwhile for a period of at least six months?

If the answer is no, reconsider the purchase.

3. Do you really need to make this purchase or are you doing it for other reasons such as to impress others (including those who you may not respect but just envy)?

4. Is there a better use you could make of this money such as saving it for a bigger goal, investing it for the future or giving some of it to help others in greater need?

5. Do you have room to store or keep what you're purchasing or will you need to rent, find additional space or clear out other items to keep it?

6. How does your purchase affect the environment?

What irreplaceable resources in the world will be used up if you make this purchase? Think about all the steps that need to be taken to manufacture, sell and transport your purchase. Your small actions all add up.

9. Frugality

You may define "frugal" as being "cheap." The dictionary defines "frugal" as "reflecting economy in the expenditure of resources."

Our notion of frugality has been shaped very much by Ebenezer Scrooge of Charles Dickens' "A Christmas Carol." Scrooge only allowed his assistant one piece of coal to warm himself while working. Scrooge wasn't frugal. He was cheap.

Frugality doesn't mean being cheap. It means becoming a more conscious shopper and consumer and looking for ways to save money. For example, you can be frugal by buying generic brands (where the quality is no different) or by shopping at sales whenever possible.

10. Short- and long-term goals

Meeting short-term as compared to long-term goals is a constant battle when it comes to money.

Very often, it's a question of satisfying many short-term goals (e.g., to get the latest CD, DVD, MP3 player or video game system) or putting all or most of them on hold to save up for a more expensive goal (e.g., computer, car, college expenses or a house).

Develop your skills in saving and investing to meet your long-term goals. See the big picture to get the willpower to work towards your long-term goals.

PART TWO
Money-Smart Ways
to Live Day to Day

11. Practice safe Net on
social networking sites

Social networking sites are a great way to meet people—people you like and people you'd rather never meet online or offline.

Be careful about your online postings for a couple of reasons. First, if you post too much identifying information, you could be putting your physical safety in jeopardy. Along the same lines, that information could be used for identity theft by helping a criminal piece together more of your personal information.

Finally, it is becoming more common for university admissions officers and employers to do online searches to see what you've posted on your hobbies, interests and other extracurricular activities.

A rule of thumb is that if you wouldn't want a school or employer to see what you posted online, don't put it out there for the world to see.

One extra word of caution here. Whenever you post anything on the Net, you lose control of it. You may think you can post anything today and then delete it down the road before you apply to college or enter the workforce. What you may not be aware of is that there are companies already in the business of archiving Web pages and saving old versions of websites. That could include social networking sites.

It would be a shame to lose a chance for that college opportunity or dream job in the future because of an inappropriate posting today. Think about it.

12. Protect your cellphone, computer and yourself

Below are some basic steps you can take to protect yourself. If you want more detailed information on how to better protect your computer and your mobile devices, see if your library has a softcover or e-book edition of my book, *Teach Your Computer to Dance: Make Your Computer, Mobile Devices and the Internet Perform for You.*

At a minimum, you should do the following:

Be careful when you set up your IM (instant messaging)

Make sure you restrict users to just your buddy list. Unless absolutely needed, keep it simple and disable advanced features, file sharing and the file transfer features. Also, since instant messaging in general is not the most secure way of communicating, you may want to have a program to help keep your instant messages confidential and provide protection against unauthorized inbound and outbound IM traffic.

Use Bluetooth wisely

Bluetooth offers short-range wireless connectivity between a cellphone and a headset, a computer and a printer or a mobile device and a computer.

Bluetooth generally broadcasts up to 30 feet. However, hackers can extend the range to 300 feet or sometimes up to a mile.

That's why you want to link up (pair) devices in private; avoid linking up with strangers; keep your device in a nondiscoverable (hidden) mode when Bluetooth is on; have a complex password and turn Bluetooth off when you're not using it. For more information on how to better protect yourself using Bluetooth, see *Teach Your Computer to Dance.*

Don't be casual with your passwords

If your passwords are easy to crack or accessible to others, you're asking for trouble.

Give some thought and use some imagination in setting up your passwords for your mobile devices and your computer. Here are some essential guidelines:

1. Passwords should *not* contain real words, actual names, addresses, phone numbers or birth dates.

2. Use more complex passwords (ideally, a combination of at least eight to 11 upper and lower-case letters, numbers *and* keyboard symbols) to give greater security to your passwords.

3. Change your passwords at least several times a year.

4. Use different passwords for different sites, programs and devices.

Be cautious with downloads

Avoid opening up files attached to IMs or emails from senders you do not know. Those files are a great way to infect your computer or mobile device. Scan every download using antivirus software.

Links can be dangerous

Avoid clicking on any links in IMs or emails because you may be misdirected to a dangerous site posing as a real site (phishing). Instead, type in the URL yourself.

Hot spots may be more dangerous than you think

You may use a wireless (e.g., Wi-Fi) connection at a hot spot (e.g., coffee shop). Remember that Wi-Fi is a shared network. Be aware that fellow customers may be more interested in your information than a caffeine buzz. With their laptop computers, they may be trying to monitor the Wi-Fi radio waves from your device to capture your information, passwords and credit card information.

Some hot spots have better security protection than others. That's why as a first line of defense, try to minimize your use of hot spots, especially if you're dealing with sensitive information. In particular, try to avoid using instant messaging at hot spots since this is not the most secure method of communicating. When not in use, turn off your wireless card.

For more information on making yourself safer at hot spots, see *Teach Your Computer to Dance*.

Lower your profile on the Net

Make yourself less of a visible target. For example, if you have an "always on" connection to the Internet such as through DSL or a cable modem, you're increasing the chances that someone will find your connection and attack it at that time or at their leisure since your connection is always sitting there. Disconnect your high-speed modem when you're not on the Internet.

Keep your computer's operating system up to date

The operating system for every computer needs to get security updates from time to time. You can probably enable automatic updates from the software manufacturer.

Keep your Internet browser and other software up to date

Go to the website of your Internet browser and the providers of your main software applications (e.g., word processing, DVD burning and video editing software) periodically to make sure you have the latest updates on your computer to prevent security breaches.

Use antivirus, antispam, antispyware and pop-up blocker programs or possibly a security suite to protect yourself

There's a lot more you can do to protect yourself. You'll want to have one antivirus program, one antispam program, one pop-up blocker and several antispyware programs. Every week scan your computer using your antivirus and antispyware programs.

Install a router that has a built-in hardware firewall

A router is a piece of hardware. Your computer's modem gets plugged into it. A router that's part of your Internet connection acts just like a high fence that's around your home. Just like a fence, it can make it more difficult for a stranger to see what's behind the barrier (your computer) and to go after what's being protected. Some fences are more protective than others and some do a better job of completely concealing what's hidden behind the fence. Routers with built-in hardware firewalls are like that, too.

Routers can be used with modems from many computers at once or with just one computer.

To help keep hackers out, change the factory default password to maintain control over your router.

Make your wireless router and network more secure

Routers can be hard-wired or wireless. With computers, wired connections are generally more secure than wireless connections. Many wireless (Wi-Fi) routers come with no security features made active. The default setting can leave you defenseless. Newer routers may make it easier to secure your network and Internet connections.

If you have a wireless network, have the security settings activated at every access point and at the highest level (e.g., WPA security is more protective than WEP security and WPA2 should be more protective than WPA) and use a secure passphrase (password), too.

Change the name of your wireless network rather than using a default name familiar to hackers.

Restrict the strength of your wireless network's signal. The stronger your wireless signal, the greater the likelihood that outsiders can tap into it. Adjust the signal strength so it's just enough to reach each access point and no more. Locate access points in central locations away from windows and outside walls.

Use a software firewall, too

A software firewall is a software program that, like a hardware firewall, helps protect what goes in your computer. It also controls what comes out. How many software firewalls are enough? One. With more than one, the software programs may conflict with one another. Keep your firewall up to date by installing updates, as needed.

13. Electronics and your life

TV, more so than other electronics, may be costing you more than you think.

Hard as it may be to believe, even with the competition from MP3 players, video games, PC games, cellphones and IMing, the average amount of time spent by your age group each day watching TV went up last year.

Do you want to spend 10 years of your life watching TV?

If you watch an average of three hours of TV a day, seven days a week, you're "spending" over 1,000 hours a year in front of the tube. Over a lifetime of 80 years, that's 10 years of your life spent watching TV.

Am I making up this math? Calculate the numbers yourself. Three hours of TV a day equals 1/8 of a 24-hour day. If you live 80 years, 1/8 of that time span is 10 years.

Reduce TV watching from even three hours to two hours a day and that's over three years of additional free time for you during your lifetime. Better yet, follow the second best advice in this book (the best advice is in Money-Smart Way #32) — take that extra hour per day and read *The Wall Street Journal*, a newspaper that covers money matters and more importantly, the world.

No matter how much you enjoy TV, is it worth 10 years of your life? If commercials take up about 15 to 20 minutes of each TV hour, you could be spending three solid years of your life watching commercials.

How TV is different

TV is a different form of electronics. It's more of a passive, often solo activity with no interaction by you except to watch, press the remote control and absorb the content—including commercials that take over the *entire screen*. With media spreading to every device, sometimes you're forced to sit through *pre-rolls*—the commercials that come before many Web videos.

Of course, chances are good that while you're watching TV, you're multitasking—probably with your other electronics.

Many other electronics (except single-player PC or video games) can also be a social activity with virtual or forms of real interaction (IMs, audio or video comments to one another).

One of the best ways to find extra time, improve yourself or the world, save money and reduce your "wants" is to stop watching TV—on your TV, cellphone or video MP3 player.

Since that's not likely, read on for two tips that may be an acceptable compromise.

TV temptation

TV is designed to:

- make you want to buy what's advertised
- make you believe your life will change if you buy what's advertised
- convince you that you will be like the actors in TV commercials if you buy what's being advertised
- give you the irresistible urge to buy and consume (that's why we're called consumers)

- most sadly, make you feel incomplete or inadequate if you don't own what's being advertised.

Commercials are hard for everyone to resist. After all, they're designed by professionals whose job is to convince us we can't live without the advertised product or service.

These advertising pros also have the benefit of market research (trying out ideas or approaches on small groups of people before you see the final ad) to see which keywords and images will cause us to salivate and be compelled to buy. Add to that the repetition of ads and the day-to-day exposure of seeing our peers who've purchased advertised products and it's hard for anyone to resist TV temptation.

Two ways to beat the advertising pros

Your fingers might outwit the advertising professionals by using the mute button during commercials. Although watching a commercial in silence will still have some impact, you greatly reduce the advertising power of the ad.

Another alternative is just to stop watching commercials by immediately switching to another program (but not another commercial) or using today's technology to skip over commercials.

14. Notebook riches

It's easy to lose track of time when you're involved with your electronics. It's also easy to lose track of your money as you spend it. Do you know where your money is? Do you know how you're spending it?

To get and keep day-to-day control of your money and know where it's going, you need to take two steps.

First, carry around a small notebook for one month and write down every single penny you spend. You'll be amazed at where your money goes and you'll discover easy ways to save extra money each day.

This will help you when you sit down and take the second step of prioritizing (ranking) your spending goals (see Money-Smart Way #15).

15. Getting a handle on day-to-day spending

Do you have enough money to meet all your spending needs? The way to accomplish this is to prioritize your goals and spend your money by keeping your most important goals in mind.

Having goals in mind helps you with both day-to-day and long-term, larger expenditures. It gives you a way to see whether spending decisions make sense for what's really important to you.

The "right" way for you to spend your money

The right spending decisions are different for everyone. What someone else thinks is a good use of money may not be what you think.

Create your own spending plan

You need to create *your own plan* for spending. With a plan, you can avoid impulsive spending, which is where you spend without thinking about your most important goals.

Five steps to get a handle on day-to-day spending

1. Make a list of your short- and long-term life goals.

As baseball star Yogi Berra once said, "If you don't know where you're going, you won't know when you get there." Writing down your goals makes them more real to you.

2. Track your spending and match it with what you have to spend.

Before the start of each month, make a list of the money you expect to receive and what you expect to spend. After the month ends, compare the actual results with what you expected. See where you need to make changes for the next month.

If you don't have enough money to spend on everything you want (or need), where do you cut back? Some expenses are required such as car insurance. Other expenditures such as eating out are optional and can be cut back.

By using the expense notebook in Money-Smart Way #14 and looking at expenses as either required or optional, you'll begin to see your spending habits.

3. Spend (or save) your money first on your most important goals.

Take a sheet of paper and divide it into three columns that you label "#1," "#2" and "#3." Now rank your expenditures in categories of importance from #1 through #3. For example, #1 priorities are your most important goals (e.g., paying car insurance, saving for a new computer, a car or for college). #2 priorities are not as critical (e.g., buying extra clothes) and #3 priorities are the least important ones (e.g., buying soft drinks).

Try to meet your #1 priorities to the greatest extent possible before spending on #2 and #3 priorities.

4. Become a smart spender.

There's more on this in Money-Smart Way #16 and later in Part Three: Money-Smart Ways to Shop.

5. Review your goals every year.

At the end of each year, see how well you did in meeting your goals and make a new list for the next year.

16. Ten ways to become an everyday money-smart spender

When you spend, you expend (use up). You may be using up more than money. You're using up the work (time and energy) required to earn the money.

Spending is more than the act of handing over dollar bills, a check, a debit card or a credit card. It's also handing over a part of you. With this in mind, here are 10 great ways to become an everyday money-smart spender. All of these small items can add up big.

1. When in doubt about a purchase, don't buy it.

2. Every day try to cut down on expenses in some way.

Buy a soft drink or coffee every other day rather than every day (besides saving money, you'll improve your health).

3. Reduce your entertainment costs. Instead of spending full price for every movie you see, for half of them go to a matinee, a bargain theatre or see them on rental DVDs. Trade in movie and game DVDs to get cash or credit against future purchases.

4. Eat at home or pack a meal for half the times you'd usually eat out.

5. Shop during sales.

6. Use coupons.

7. Check out books and music at your library.

8. Shop with a list in hand and stick to it.

9. Try to repair an item before buying a replacement.

10. Consider buying used rather than new items. The cost savings can be big, especially with cars.

Even small steps can add up to hundreds of thousands of dollars over your lifetime through the power of compound growth (Money-Smart Way #69).

17. The art of asking questions

Whether you're calling customer service about a problem with your computer or a salesperson to get product information, learn to ask questions and to keep asking them until you get the answers you want and understand.

If you don't understand an answer, don't blame yourself. Chances are good the explanation wasn't clear enough. Don't be afraid or embarrassed to ask again saying, "I didn't quite understand. Could you please explain it again another way?"

Then, once you feel it's clear to you, you may want to say, "Let me say it back to you in my own words to make sure I got it right."

Be sure to take notes when you ask questions by writing down the item you're calling about, the name (and employee number) of the person you're speaking to, their position, the phone number you called, the date and time you called, your questions and the answers given. Have a notebook or folder where you keep these notes organized.

Then, later on, if you have a problem, you'll be in a better position to back up your understanding of what was said to you.

If it's really important, confirm what a company representative or salesperson says to you by emailing, faxing or mailing a letter. Think about including a sentence such as "If anything I've written is incorrect, please advise me immediately by phone and in writing." Keep a copy of whatever you write. You may also ask them to email, fax or write you back to confirm what you wrote is correct.

Then if what you see, talked about or purchased isn't what you thought it should be, you'll be better able to document your claims in writing.

18. Cash register smarts

Whether you're making a purchase in a grocery store, video store, department store or an amusement park, pay attention.

Watch the scanner

Mistakes can happen when scanners are used to record purchases. Sometimes an item is scanned twice or a clerk accidentally punches in the incorrect quantity for an item. Other times, the wrong price is programmed into the checkout register.

As your purchases are being scanned in, keep an eye on the amount actually being charged.

Double-check your receipt right away

Before you leave a store, always look at your receipt. Be aware or you may pay (sometimes twice).

19. Some tips on tipping

The reason to tip is to reward the quality of the service you receive.

Since tipping is most often done in a restaurant, here are some guidelines.

First, check the bill to make sure the items and prices are listed correctly. Then, see whether a tip has *already* been included in the bill (this is more common when there is a group of six or more eating together).

Standard, acceptable service is usually tipped at 15%. There are two schools of thought on whether the 15% should apply to (1) the charges without tax or (2) the charges plus tax. You can decide on what's right for you. The second alternative adds about 1% to the tip.

Sometimes, you'll want to tip extra (a 20% tip instead of 15%) for especially good service. Other times, you'll leave a much smaller tip or no tip at all if the service was very poor.

Remember that tips are not to be paid automatically. You're rewarding the level of service you received.

PART THREE
Money-Smart Ways to Shop

20. Doubling your money while shopping

Saving money while shopping can be a two-for-one deal for you.

Every dollar may be worth two dollars. Here's why. Because of federal and state income taxes, Social Security and Medicare taxes, you (or more likely your parents) may need to earn nearly two dollars for every dollar you spend. So, every dollar you save when you shop can mean two dollars in benefits to you. Every $100 you save this way can be like earning $200.

But keep in mind that you are *not* making money even when you reduce your shopping expenses. You're spending money and hopefully looking for ways to save when you shop.

21. Get real when you shop

The next time you go shopping, pretend you're living in the Middle Ages and you've gone to a marketplace to trade or barter.

Instead of having brought your crops or your cattle with you, you've lugged your cash, checks, ATM card, debit card or credit card to the marketplace. How you pay for your purchases will have a big impact on how much you spend.

Buying on plastic makes purchases unreal

When a credit card is used to make a purchase, it doesn't feel like someone opened up your wallet or pocketbook and took money out of it. If it did feel that way, you would tend to spend less (and save more). Why is that?

With a credit card purchase, what feels real is walking out of the store with an armful of goodies. And to think you got all that stuff just for signing your name to a piece of paper that's a credit card slip! The reality of the cost of a credit card purchase only hits you when your credit card statement arrives weeks later in the mail.

The unreality of spending with credit cards becomes more apparent when you compare it to spending by cash or a check (a debit card feels like a mix of a credit card and a check).

Paying by cash feels real and saves you money

Paying by cash is as real as it gets with spending. It's like trading the cow you brought to market in return for the goods you'll carry home.

You'd notice a missing cow and the same thing happens when you pay by cash. As you hand over the bills to the merchant and your wallet or pocketbook becomes skinnier, the transaction becomes real and physical to you and your brain.

That is why people who pay only by cash spend less than people who pay by check, debit card or credit card. Paying with cash also helps you avoid debt by allowing you to spend only what you have on hand and in hand.

Naturally, cash can't be used for every purchase (and shouldn't be such as where you may later want proof of payment with a cancelled check or where you can get a free extended warranty through a credit card purchase).

Try to use cash as often as possible as a technique to reduce your spending. If you're using an ATM card to get that cash, make sure you leave enough money in your account to pay for your other expenses.

Paying by check also helps keep reality in mind

If you write down every check and every deposit in your checkbook register (or keep track of it through your online checking account) and keep a running total of the balance on hand, you'll stay in touch with financial reality.

If you don't write a check for more than your checking account balance on hand, you have a way to control your spending and make the impact of spending seem more real.

Debit cards

With a debit card that automatically reduces your checking account balance for each purchase, you're more tied into financial reality.

However, the physical act of filling out a check is more real and time consuming than just signing your name on a debit card purchase. Signing a debit card slip is similar to signing a credit card slip. It doesn't quite create the same mental impact as a check to indicate to yourself that you've really got fewer funds on hand after the purchase. (Also see Money-Smart Way #39 on why using debit cards may give less protection than credit cards.)

Coming back to reality

When you shop, you need to be aware of what you can afford to spend. Credit cards remove that reality. What you have with credit cards is an available balance to *spend*, *not* an available ability to *pay*.

Using cash and checks can better give you that reality check. Both of these ways make you more aware of what money you really have to spend.

Make shopping more real and you'll lower your expenses, lessen your stress and have greater flexibility in your life through increased financial independence.

Credit cards can have their benefits, too. See Money-Smart Way #29 to see how you may be able to extend the warranty on a purchase by using a credit card and Money-Smart Way #30 on how credit cards better protect you on returning purchases.

22. Know why you're shopping

If you want to control your shopping, shop with a specific purchase (and purpose) in mind. Shop with a purpose by having a shopping list in hand before you walk out your door.

23. Shop with a budget

When you shop, you need to budget, too. When you budget, you match up the money you have and what you are doing with it. In general, you have four options with your money:

1. Buy things now

2. Save to buy things another day

3. Save and invest

4. Give to charity

It's a natural instinct to spend money as soon as it's received. For some reason, this usually leads to running out of money too soon.

At some point, you'll need to control your everyday spending so you can save up to make a bigger purchase such as an MP3 player, a video game system, a computer, a car or a house.

Putting aside money for future purchases is part of budgeting. Learn to budget now and you'll have a lifetime tool that will keep you out of money trouble.

Remember the distinction between needs and wants in Money-Smart Way #4. It really comes into play when making a budget.

What is a budget? It's a way of making sure you have enough money on hand for what's really important to you. It's a way to pay for your needs and hopefully, some of your wants, too.

Four steps to a good budget

1. Write down your expected income (that might be your allowance as well as your earnings).

Start doing budgets for one week at a time and work your way up to doing two-week and then monthly budgets. Eventually, you'll be doing yearly budgets.

2. Then make a list of your expected spending for the budget period you selected in #1 above.

Write down your spending in five categories for using your money: what you really need to spend now, how much you'd like to save, what you'd like to spend in the future, what you'd like to give to others and what you'd like to spend on your wants (see Money-Smart Way #4).

3. Make sure #1 (income) is bigger than #2 (spending) or else you'll need to earn some extra money or cut down on your spending.

4. Learn how to control short-term spending.

It can be tough to add extra income especially if you're going to school and already working part-time. So, the primary budgeting skill you need to develop now is how to cut down on short-term spending. If you want to save enough for a major purchase such as a car without going into any or too much debt, you'll need to control spending on short-term wants.

Stay within your budget to find the right balance for using your money.

24. Avoid impulsive spending

The best budget is useless if you do too much impulsive spending. These unplanned purchases are not part of your budget (unless you've planned for a certain amount of "unplanned" spending).

To avoid impulsive spending, you need special protective armor. Since you are continually subjected to advertisements encouraging you to buy more, it's hard to resist impulsive shopping. We live in a society that is constantly pushing us to spend, whether we can afford it or not.

Protect yourself against impulsive spending by budgeting your spending in advance and sticking to your budget.

25. Shopping is not like breathing

Fortunately, you could survive for quite a while if you put your shopping on hold. We are all often unaware of our reasons for shopping and so it helps to become more conscious of why we shop (especially for things we really don't need). Some people use shopping as a way to cheer themselves up or as a form of entertainment.

If you often go shopping (and spending), try instead to develop other forms of social interaction and recreation. Being with friends or family, exercising, enjoying nature, reading a good book from the library or volunteering to help others can be a far more profitable use of your time.

26. Four times not to shop

Thursday, Friday, Saturday and Sunday. Seriously, here are four times you shouldn't be shopping:

1. If you're depressed or feeling low, it's too easy to make unnecessary purchases.

2. If you can get something for free, don't pay for it.

Good examples are books and movie DVDs. Very often, you'll read a book once or see a movie DVD once and never look at it again except to try to find a place to store it. Then, over the years, you'll spend more time and money moving these never-to-be-read-again books and never-to-be-seen-again movies with you as you crisscross the country.

Think instead about just borrowing a book or DVD from the library or a friend. Another great way to view movie DVDs is through the monthly plans where you order on the Net and then have movies delivered through the mail. Then, if you feel you really want the book or movie as part of your permanent collection, you can always buy it (and *then* lug it everywhere you move to).

3. If you're just trying to impress someone else with a purchase you want to make, save your money and figure out how to improve your self-esteem instead.

4. If you really can't afford to go shopping for an item, don't. Be realistic as to what's affordable and what's really a burden to buy.

27. Nine steps to successful shopping

Here are nine steps to help make your shopping successful. To put them in a context, as you go through the steps, think about how they would apply to the purchase of a computer.

1. Do comparison shopping

One of the keys to being a money-smart shopper is to do comparison shopping. Zero in on what you need. Do research online and through magazines, stores and friends to determine the specifications you need and the product reviews of the various choices.

Comparison shopping falls into two categories: (1) comparing apples to apples and (2) comparing apples to oranges. Also see Money-Smart Way #28.

Compare apples to apples

If you definitely know the exact item (e.g., model number) you want to purchase, you can then compare prices on the Internet or call different stores.

To make sure you're really comparing the exact same product (e.g., apples to apples), be sure to ask about shipping costs, warranties and return policies, too. What may appear to be less expensive at first may change once you get the whole story.

If possible, personally take a look at what you'll be buying.

Comparing apples and oranges

You may not be sure exactly which product you want to buy. Here's where it gets trickier to do comparison shopping.

Very often, products only list some of their features. It can be difficult to know what's included and excluded on products of a similar type. You can get much of the needed information through the Net or at your local library. Also try calling a toll-free customer service number to ask your questions and see whether there are some specification or "spec" sheets on the Net that list *and* compare features on different products.

Then, once you've decided on a particular product, you can then go back to your apples-to-apples comparison shopping.

2. Buy pre-owned

Second, consider buying pre-owned rather than new products. Since just about everyone prefers buying new to old, why buy pre-owned (a fancy word for used)? Buying used saves money.

And in many cases, the quality is the same. You can buy a used, unscratched CD or DVD and the quality can be as clear as a new one. If you can buy a refurbished computer, it may be of the same quality and have the same warranty as a new computer. The only difference might be in the price—it's lower. However, if your warranty is automatically extended by using your credit card, that extension may not apply to refurbished computers—ask your credit card company.

Libraries are a great way to save on book costs. And once you're in college, look for other ways to save money on textbooks, including shopping on the Net and/or buying used textbooks or e-books.

There are other reasons to consider buying pre-owned products. You may be helping the environment by keeping a product in use that might otherwise go into an overcrowded landfill. Buying used may keep valuable natural resources from being used up to produce, transport and sell a new product.

If it bothers you to buy something used, consider getting the product through a trade or barter with friends instead. You may have clothes, a CD, DVD, MP3 or DVD player or a computer that is no longer right for you. Maybe it's the right fit for friends of yours and they'll have something you need in return.

Just remember there is a big problem when you buy something new. Right away it becomes "used" anyway. That's the reason you hear a new car loses thousands of dollars of value as soon as it's driven off the lot.

3. Shop at sales

Some of the best sales are during the off season. For example, once winter ends, winter clothes go down in price. You can be dollars ahead for next year by making next year's purchases during this year's off-season sale.

Department stores have certain items that go on sale during a certain month of the year. Call the major stores close to you and ask about their schedule of sales for the upcoming year. It may be worth waiting to make a purchase until the sale month comes up for that product.

One last word about sales. Sometimes special sale prices only apply to certain items and not the ones of interest to you.

4. Save with newspaper (or Internet) coupons

You can save money with newspapers in two main ways. Sales are often advertised in papers. In addition, newspapers are filled with coupons (also see Money-Smart Way #28 on Internet coupons). Some stores honor coupons from competitors' stores or the Net. Remember, a coupon doesn't save you money unless you really need the item. But if you do, coupons can be a great way to save.

5. Keep ads to show special prices

Sometimes you go to a store in response to an ad only to find the price of a product is higher than advertised. Usually, this is an oversight on the part of the merchant. One way of getting the special advertised price is to bring the advertisement to the store so any difference in the price will be resolved in your favor. Bringing an ad with you to a store is another way of having a shopping list to control your spending.

6. Get value for your purchases

Good shopping means getting your money's worth, not just spending as little as you can.

One of the toughest tasks is learning how to judge quality and value. Usually, quality purchases mean items that will last longer and cost more. With some purchases, it means more durability or strength. With others, it may mean that they won't become outdated as soon.

Quality takes on other aspects in other parts of our lives. For example, in a grocery store, getting good value may depend on your reading product labels to determine which product is better.

7. Learn to negotiate

Although we don't shop in a bazaar where bartering or price haggling is the usual way to buy, the savvy shopper, knowing there may be plenty of room to negotiate, doesn't necessarily accept prices at face value.

Think about it. You'll often see advertisements that say, "We'll match any advertised price." That means that the listed prices in the store may be higher than the competition's and the store doesn't want to lose your business to a competitor. If stores are in essence advertising that their prices will be lower if you ask, speak up.

Don't be afraid to make an offer if you feel a price for a purchase is too high or unaffordable for you. Just say to the merchant, the car rental agency, the hotel or any other seller, "What's the best price you can give me?" or "I can only afford this much." The worst they can say is no. You've got a chance that they'll say yes or settle somewhere in the middle. Why overpay? If you can spot a defect, even a small one, in a product you may also be better able to negotiate a lower price.

Don't overlook the Internet in hunting for bargains. You may decide to make purchases over the Internet or you may use the information you've obtained there to negotiate with your local stores. By being able to show them a printout of how little you can spend for the same item over the Net, you may receive an instant discount to encourage you to make the purchase from them.

8. Ask for a cash discount

If you're paying by cash, you're saving the merchant money. On every credit card transaction, a merchant has to pay the credit card company 2 or 3% as a credit card fee. Why not pocket that discount yourself? Ask for a cash discount.

9. Learn to say no

The most effective negotiating technique is being able to say no and mean it. If you're ready to walk away from a transaction but the other side wants you to stay, you definitely can have the upper hand. This allows you to get a better price or to just pass on the transaction if it really doesn't make sense for you.

28. Shopping smart on the Internet

Here are six ways to be a money-smart shopper on the Internet:

1. Use price-comparison and research sites

Use more than one shopping site to search around for price comparisons and to see how merchants are rated for service and reliability.

Shopping Research/Price-Comparison Sites

Become.com is a shopping research and price comparison service that includes buying guides, consumer reviews, articles, specifications, forums and comparison pricing information. Over seven million products are available. You'll also see searches other Become users have performed, real-time suggestions from the site on search terms you may want to use and news (and links) from top U.S. news sources related to your shopping. Become, Inc., *www.become.com*

Bizrate.com is a shopping search site that uses price, popularity, product availability and merchant reputation for its ranking system. Their index includes over 30 million products from more than 40,000 stores. Shopzilla, Inc., *www.bizrate.com*

Buysafeshopping.com offers more than two million items including listings from eBay and Overstock.com auctions. buySAFE, Inc., *www.buysafeshopping.com*

Complaints.com airs consumer grievances. You might want to check it out before you make your next purchase. Sagacity Corp., *www.complaints.com*

Google Product Search is Google's shopping search engine. Google, Inc., *www.google.com/products*

MyRatePlan.com lets you compare cellphone plans to find what's best for you and/or your family. MyRatePlan.com, LLC, *www.MyRatePlan.com*

MySimon is a well-known shopping search engine. CNET Networks, Inc., *www.mysimon.com*

PriceGrabber.com offers price comparisons, product reviews and side-by-side product comparisons. Pricegrabber.com, LLC, *www.pricegrabber.com*

PriceRunner is a top-rated price guide and shopping comparison site. Pricerunner, *www.pricerunner.com*

PriceWatch is a street price search engine for computer components and peripherals. *www.pricewatch.com*

Shopping.com has millions of products, thousands of merchants and millions of reviews from the Epinions community. eBay, Inc., *www.shopping.com*

2. Use Internet coupons

Look for Internet coupons and get other money-saving ideas from the Internet.

Coupon Sites

Fatwallet, FatWallet, Inc., *www.fatwallet.com*

GottaDeal, OlsenNet LLC, *www.gottadeal.com*

3. Online auctions

Online auction sites might have what you need at the right price for you.

4. Look at sources off the Net

Use consumer magazines available at your library to compare the information you get on the Net. Also, the U.S. government has a free Consumer Information Catalog listing more than 200 free and low-cost federal publications on many subjects. To view/receive the catalog, log on to *www.pueblo.gsa.gov* or call 888-878-3256.

5. Have a purpose to your shopping before you start surfing

A great way to spend too much money is to go spending without a specific purchase in mind. That way, everything looks good to buy!

6. Be careful in providing information

Be cautious in providing a credit card number and other personal information over the Net (or by phone or mail). See Money-Smart Way #40 on Preventing Identity Theft.

29. Warranties

Products (and sometimes services) come with warranties. Warranties are guarantees that usually last for a certain period of time. Some warranties are written out on the box or an insert when you buy a product. Others are part of the general laws of your state or the U.S.

The point is you may have more rights than you think if something goes wrong with a product. If there's a problem, first look at the written warranty that came with the product.

Depending on how organized you are, you could have a problem finding your warranty information. Keep track of your warranty information by creating one file folder called "Warranties." In the file, have a summary sheet as the top sheet with columns for the:

- item purchased

- date purchased

- place purchased

- length of standard warranty

- length of any extra warranty (you may have purchased an

extended warranty or you may automatically have one if you used a credit card to make the purchase — check with your credit card company before making a major purchase to see if you'll receive a free extended warranty through the credit card company — sometimes these extended warranties do not include refurbished items)

Put the latest purchase paperwork and receipt (or a copy) right below the summary sheet so it's in reverse chronological order with the most recent purchases on top.

Then, the next time something breaks down, just scan down your summary sheet at the top of the file to see if you're still covered by the warranty.

30. How to protect yourself when returning purchases

Before you make a purchase, find out the merchant's return policy.

For nondefective items, you may have to pay shipping and handling charges and sometimes also a "restocking fee" of 10-20% to return an item.

Even returning defective products does not always go smoothly. It is usually wise to have muscle in your corner to back you up if something goes wrong with a purchase.

You can get more of that protection by purchasing with a credit card. If merchandise is not delivered or is defective, your credit card company may assist you in getting the right merchandise, a refund of your money or reversing the charge on your credit card.

By contrast, if you pay by check and the check has cleared a checking account, getting a refund may involve hiring an attorney. That's probably too expensive. And sellers of defective or undelivered merchandise may disappear or go out of business too quickly to allow you to get a refund anyway.

PART FOUR
Money-Smart Ways to Handle Debt and Credit

31. Keeping good credit—what's in it for you?

Just as you use a passport to identify yourself to enter another country, your *credit report* and your *credit score* identify you to lenders, employers, landlords and others who want to know more about you. It's not the only tool they use to judge you, but it is a common one.

Credit report vs. credit score

A *credit report* is a dollars and cents report that shows how well (or poorly) you've been doing in paying your bills, how much debt you've taken on and how long you've had the debt. This type of report contains a lot of specific dollar details as well as public information records such as bankruptcies and tax liens.

The three main credit reporting agencies are:

- Equifax, *www.equifax.com*

- Experian, *www.experian.com*

- TransUnion, *www.tuc.com*

A *credit score* is a three-digit number (higher is better) that lenders and others use to help them determine whether you're a good credit risk. Also known as *risk scores*, the most widely used one is the *FICO* from Fair Isaac (*www.myfico.com*). The three credit reporting agencies also offer a credit score. There is generally a fee for receiving your credit score.

Very often, employers, insurance companies, landlords and others will want to see your credit report and your credit score to assess your reliability.

Incentive to pay bills on time and control spending

If you start out your life paying your bills on time and keep doing so, you'll be better able to qualify for loans to buy a car, electronics or purchase a home. Not only will good credit allow you to qualify to get bigger loans to make these purchases, you may get them on better terms (e.g., at a lower interest rate).

Keep your financial house in order from the beginning and your life will go much more smoothly over time.

Because how you take care of your credit is a reflection of your financial trustworthiness, a good credit record can also mean lower insurance costs and getting better jobs.

If you have trouble paying your bills on time, don't ignore the bills. Instead, call up your creditors (the people/companies you owe) and let them know your situation. They may be able to offer a different payment schedule or interest rate that you can meet to keep your credit record in good shape.

How does someone find out your credit record?

The credit reporting agencies provide credit reports about you. Once you've entered the world of being a bill payer or borrower, it's a good idea once a year to look at your credit reports from credit reporting agencies to make sure the information listed there is accurate. If anything is incorrect, advise the reporting agency.

You can get one free copy of your credit report from each of the credit reporting agencies—Equifax, Experian and TransUnion—once a year. You don't have to request the report from each agency at the same time. You could space it out every four months so you're always keeping an eye on your credit report and in a better position to timely correct any mistakes in a report.

It's also a good idea to get your reports in order several months before you plan any action or transaction that will involve providing a credit report on you to make sure everything is accurate.

At some point you may also decide to sign up for a *credit monitoring service* so you know when there's activity affecting your credit report and/or credit score.

What affects your credit score?

Be aware that you may have different credit scores from each credit reporting agency.

Your credit score is determined by many factors including your on time (or delinquent) track record in making payments; your involvement in lawsuits, bankruptcies or foreclosures; the amount of your debt; the types of debts (credit cards, installment loans, mortgages, etc.); whether you're taking on new debt now; how many credit-related accounts you have; the length of your credit history; and, to some degree, the number of inquiries by lenders. For more information on credit scores, go to *www.myfico.com*.

32. The best credit card advice

If you take one piece of advice from this book, it's this — avoid credit card debt.

Credit card debt can be a ball and chain following you around, everywhere you go, for years and years. Too many students are graduating college with a diploma and student loan bills in one hand and credit card bills in the other.

It's so easy to use the plastic to make a purchase that you'll pay for tomorrow and next week and maybe for years to come. As you'll see in Money-Smart Way #33, the interest rate you're paying on credit card debt may be much higher than you think.

So if you use a credit card, be ready to pay off your balance in full before the due date to avoid interest and penalties. If that is not possible, try not to make any other credit card purchases until you've saved enough to pay off the existing credit card balance (along with any additional interest due).

Life went on before credit cards were first used in the 1950s. Now made of plastic, they were originally made of sheets of paper pasted together. Credit cards changed how people shop and spend. With a credit card, people could spend money they didn't have yet but that they expected (or hoped) to have in the future. Having a credit card feels like you own a printing press to print money but it's really a printing press to create bills.

33. What credit card interest really costs

Ben Franklin was only half right when he said, "A penny saved is a penny earned." He didn't have to deal with income tax. I wonder what the Boston Tea Party would have been like if our Founding Fathers had to fill out today's income tax returns.

These days, you may need to earn up to two dollars to have one dollar left after federal and state income tax and Social Security and Medicare taxes.

The "36% return" on your investment

Interest on personal credit card debt is *not* tax deductible. Why is that important?

If you are paying 18% interest on unpaid balances, will you (or your parents) need to earn 36% on investments or earn the equivalent wages to wind up with the money to pay the 18% interest? It will depend on the applicable income tax bracket. The bottom line is that no matter what income tax bracket you are in, you are paying off credit card interest with after-tax, nondeductible dollars.

If you have to make a choice between paying off credit card debt or putting money into savings, it's *usually* better to pay off your credit card debt first (one exception might be a 401(k) plan with good employer matching contributions — see Money-Smart Way #88).

34. Having the right number of credit cards

This is one case where less is better. To avoid temptation, you should have only one credit card. In some cases, it makes sense to have a second card in case your other card is lost or stolen. That way, you wouldn't be stranded without means to pay your way.

Even if you have two cards, try for the most part to use only one of them and pay off both cards in full every month. If you are going to have an unpaid balance, use the credit card with the lower interest rate for any additional charges.

Credit card use isn't just about dollars and cents. It's about financial freedom. If you get weighed down by credit card debt, you will have tremendous stress in your life and be restricted as to the use of your time and your choices for school, jobs and housing — because you'll eventually have to pay the outstanding bills.

There's another reason not to have too many cards, especially unused cards. If you apply for a loan, the lender may reduce your loan by the amount of all of your unused credit cards since you could later access this available credit.

35. Selecting the right credit card

To find the right credit card, you need to do some shopping around. Here are the four key questions to ask:

1. Is there an annual fee whether you use the card or not?

2. What is the interest rate if you can't pay the balance in full each month?

3. If interest is due, how is the balance defined when the interest is calculated? Different cards use different methods and may define the balance differently when calculating interest. (If you pay off your credit card bill in full and on time each month, you will not pay any interest at all.)

4. How much is the penalty for late payments?

If you already have a credit card and are thinking of switching to another one that's offering a lower rate, ask some more questions. The lower rate may only apply for a short period of time. If that's the case, you may end up paying a higher rate down the road. Also, double check whether the lower rate is only for transfers of existing balances to the new card or for new purchases, too.

36. How to get out of credit card debt

If you ever find yourself up to your ears in credit card debt, you'll need a plan of action to dig your way out.

Five steps to get out of debt

1. Reduce or eliminate your credit card usage.

2. Call your existing credit card companies and ask them to reduce the current interest rate to the lowest rate they can offer you.

3. Make at least the minimum required payments and pay the most you can on the card with the highest interest rate.

4. Look for ways to cut down on expenses, even a little bit. Use this money to pay down your credit card debt.

5. Consider transferring your credit card balances to another card with a lower interest rate.

If your debt is over your head

If you want to reduce your debt or become better educated about avoiding debt, consider contacting the National Foundation for Consumer Credit (*www.nfcc.org*). This network of nonprofit organizations offers debt and budget counseling and debt repayment programs. Their services are either at no cost or a low cost.

37. Credit card statement smarts

When you get your monthly credit card statement, review it right away. First, match your receipts against the charges listed on the statement. Then double-check interest charges and any fees on it.

Four ways you may be surprised by your credit card statements

1. A merchant may have charged you more than you agreed to pay or charged you twice for the same purchase.

2. Charges from someone else's card may have ended up on your statement.

3. Someone may be using your credit card without your permission.

4. The credit card company may have charged you an incorrect interest rate or added charges that shouldn't be on the statement.

If you don't protest incorrect charges in a timely manner (usually it's within 60 days of the *date of the statement — not* 60 days from the time you received the statement — look at the rules and notices on the statement), it may be too late to avoid paying the incorrect charges.

38. Smart borrowing: the ABCs of APRs

When it comes to paying less interest on debt for the rest of your life, one term you'll need to know is *APR*.

APR is an abbreviation for *annual percentage rate*. Since it can be very difficult to compare the real cost of debt if charges are calculated differently, the APR is a way to help compare apples with apples.

When you see a loan rate, you'll usually see two rates such as 8% and 8.107% APR. It's the APR rate that is the more important rate. The purpose of the APR is to measure the true cost of a debt. That way you can see who's offering the lowest interest rate.

But don't stop there. Always find out about any other costs and fees that may be part of the transaction.

And always be sure how long the APR will stay in effect. Find out whether the rate will last six months, one year or until the debt is paid off in full.

39. Debit cards

Debit cards are an interesting mixture. They look like a credit card but they function like a check.

A debit card is really electronic money. When you use a debit card to make a purchase, the money to pay for the purchase is taken out of your account right then electronically. A debit card can be a good way to control spending since each transaction removes funds from your account.

You may use a debit card for some purchases and checks for other payments. Here's why. Sometimes merchants or tax authorities require a copy of the front and back of a cancelled check to prove that they received payment from you and they deposited your payment.

Credit cards may be better than debit cards for three reasons. If there is fraudulent activity with your card, the law provides greater protection for you with a misused credit card. Second, paying by credit card may put you in a better position to deal with defective merchandise. And, finally, your credit card company may offer extended warranties on purchases made with the credit card.

40. Preventing identity theft

You need to be careful about protecting your identity. It's getting easier for people to impersonate someone else over the phone, the Internet (IM or email) or through the mail by having essential pieces of information.

The five important parts of your identity to keep as secret as possible are your:

1. Mother's maiden name

2. Social Security number

3. Date of birth

4. Place of birth

5. Driver's license number

These pieces of your identity are most often used to prove who you say you are when conducting financial and other important transactions over the phone, through the mail or via the Internet.

When filling out forms or responding to requests for information, try to avoid giving out these pieces of information. If you must disclose your information, see if one or two of these items are enough.

PART FIVE
Money-Smart Ways to Give

41. The right time to start giving to others

In many ways, it's against human nature to take care of strangers before yourself. So should you help others and, if so, when?

How you look at charities at this time of your life may affect your view of them for a lifetime. You need to answer this question now: "When should I begin giving to charity?"

If your answer is "Once I'm wealthy enough to have leftover money after all of my needs are taken care of," you may never give to charity. Too often as income grows, so do expenses. Unless a conscious effort is made to carve out money for charity, you will never be "wealthy enough" to begin your charitable giving.

Since there are always some people worse off than you are, you can "afford" to start giving to charity long before you are rich. Not only is that the right thing to do, you will be a better person for doing it and feel good about it, too.

And your giving could be the gift of your time, not your money. Seeing the results of helping another person is one of the greatest rewards you will ever receive. Your time, effort and concern for another human being may change the course of that person's life for the better.

You may also want to consider working on a bigger scale with a cause that will help people in the U.S. or around the world to have better lives.

Start giving now. Whether it's one dollar or one hour a month, make giving a habit.

42. Getting from giving

Volunteering can pay off big for you in five main ways:

1. When you help others, you learn more about yourself and what makes you tick and feel good.

2. It doesn't hurt your resume for college, graduate school or getting a job to show your involvement with charities. In fact, the absence of charitable activities can harm your chances with potential employers or others.

3. Through charitable work, you will meet other people, good people who are volunteering like you. They may become your best friends since they share at least some of your values. Personal contacts are also one of the best ways to get ahead in the business world. People get to know you and you get to know them by working with one another on charitable activities.

4. By volunteering your time, you'll appreciate what you have and be less likely to miss what you don't have. This can help you discover the secret of being successful (see Money-Smart Way #3).

5. Volunteering will give you a broader view of the world and allow you to see how to spend your time and life energy on what really matters to you.

Get smart and start volunteering.

To find out how you can volunteer in your community, see *www.SERVEnet.org.*

Check out Youth Service America and its programs at *www.ysa.org.*

PART SIX
Money-Smart Ideas
to Discuss
with Your Parents

43. Making money agreements with your parents

Money is a very tricky subject. Some parents find it more difficult to talk about money than about any other subject. All parents want their children to be financially independent of them—both for your sake and theirs.

There may be times when you'll go to your parents for financial assistance (the polite way of saying, "I need some of your money!"). In the earlier years it may be for purchasing a DVD player, a video game system or a TV. Later on, you may need help buying a car or paying for college. Eventually, you may want to turn to your parents to help you start your own business or to buy your own home — don't count on them to lend or give you the money. Remember, they're your parents, not your banker.

If your parents do lend or give you some money, in every instance you'll be making some kind of money agreement with your parents.

It may be a silent agreement where the terms of the agreement are understood (or misunderstood) but left unspoken. It may be a loan or an arrangement where you agree to do something in return that doesn't involve repaying the money. It may call for you to do work around the house or in a family business, to get good grades or to spend time with your parents as the way to repay them.

How do you make a good money agreement with your parents?

As with any agreement or negotiation you'll encounter throughout your life, first put yourself in the other person's shoes. Ask yourself what they'll probably want from you. What would motivate them to help you? You probably can figure it out before asking them for money by thinking about what your parents will want you to do or not do in return for their help.

Once you figure out whether the motivating factor is you getting good grades, working part-time, starting to save your money or helping around the house, think about how you can fulfill your part of the agreement. Don't promise that you'll work 30 hours a week, save 90% of what you earn and keep up with your studies unless you really can and will do it. Be realistic.

Before you say what you'll do as part of the agreement, first ask your parents what they think is realistic for you to promise in return. Not only will you get a different perspective from them, you will have included them in the decision-making process and in your life. And, you will have shown them that you respect their input and advice.

For any parent, that can be a tremendous motivating force to make a money agreement with a son or daughter.

And your parents may even expect less than you were ready to offer. Then you might be able to surprise them and deliver more than you promised.

44. Making allowances for allowances

What is an allowance? No matter what your age, an allowance is your parents sharing their income or assets with you.

Depending on your parents' financial and personal circumstances and their attitudes about money and children, giving you money directly may not be possible or only a limited amount may be available for you. Some parents don't give money so their children can become more independent.

Some parents tie giving money to something being done in return (e.g., chores or working in the family business) while others give it with no strings attached.

You probably won't receive the same allowance as your friends. Every household is different. Some families have more kids, some have more money, some have special beliefs that go along with giving an allowance and some have special circumstances.

You should feel free to discuss the subject of an allowance with your parents. There's a difference between giving you money and having you earn it as your allowance. You may have one view on the subject and your parents may have another. Although there are rules of thumb on how much an allowance should be, keep in mind that some parents view allowances as gifts while others see them as payment for work or as a reward for putting in effort or achieving results in schoolwork or other areas of your life.

Allowances can take different forms. Not everyone receives money from their parents. You're receiving food, shelter, clothing and extras while living with them. That's an allowance.

Soon you may be at an age and situation where you're living outside the house but receiving assistance by borrowing a car. That's an allowance, too.

A final thought. Depending on your age and your parents' circumstances, if you are working you might consider giving them some of your earnings to help them out. What a twist—giving your parents an allowance.

45. Money, work, grades and an incentive to save

While there is much to be said in achieving just for the satisfaction of a job well done rather than to receive a reward, you may feel you deserve a reward or a bonus for good grades or for working. Different parents look at this issue differently. Your parents' outlook will be heavily influenced by their upbringing and life experiences.

Here's an idea: find out if your parents have a 401(k) retirement plan. Your parents may better relate to your request for a bonus to reward good work or good grades if they participate in a type of retirement plan at work known as a 401(k) plan.

With many 401(k) plans, employees are given an incentive to save because employers usually match some or all of the retirement savings done by the employees (your parents).

Family 401(k) plan

If you are working and saving some of your money, you may want to have a "family 401(k) plan" where your parents act like an "employer" in matching some of your savings. For example, your parents might agree that for every $100 saved by you, they'll add 20% or $20. Then, if you saved $1,000, you'd have an extra $200 from your parents.

A similar approach could be used for rewarding good grades with different levels of rewards depending on the results achieved.

46. Convincing parents you're different from your sibling(s)

You've been dealing with your parents and their money all your life. After high school or college, you may take on a different role. You may end up working in a family business or possibly contributing to household expenses through a job of your own.

At that point, you may want more financial independence or responsibility (e.g., having a credit card or access to one for which your parents are responsible). The question is whether you are ready for this next step and whether your parents are, too.

If you have siblings who have not approached their financial responsibilities in the best manner, you face the obstacle of convincing your parents that you're different from your siblings.

The best way to prove yourself to them is by living responsibly. Show your parents now that you regularly save some of your allowance or earnings. Do comparison shopping when you make purchases to show you try to save money where possible. Act responsibly with your money.

Once you establish your reliability, your parents will be more open to giving you greater access to financial responsibility.

Actions speak louder than words. Don't just tell your parents that you are different from your sibling(s). Show them.

PART SEVEN
Money-Smart Ways to Prepare for College

47. How much does it pay to go to college?

Currently, there are two financial benefits of having a four-year college degree.

First, the average yearly income for college graduates with a bachelor's degree is 50 to 75% higher than the yearly income of high school graduates.

Second, having a college degree gives you a greater choice in the work world (and maybe the romantic world) for the rest of your life. In other words, you become more desirable.

Of course, not everyone needs a college degree to be successful in life or successful financially. Especially in the Internet economy, it is possible for persons with business or advanced computer/Internet related skills to be successful without a college degree. But having a degree helps put the odds in your favor and gives you more choices and opportunities for the rest of your life.

And to keep your options open after college, keep in mind that finding the right college does involve dollars and *sense*—you don't want to have too much debt (college loans) when you leave college.

So how much does it benefit you to go to college? College means more than increasing your earning power. It's also a way to develop interests, interpersonal skills and relationships that may benefit you the rest of your life. You'll be working full-time soon enough. Don't overlook the pleasures and advantages of enjoying a college life first.

48. How to select the right college

Once you decide you want to go to college, you face thousands of choices.

Six steps to help find the right college for you

1. Determine your field of interest

Ideally, when you enter high school, start thinking about the kind of work you'll want to do after you complete college. Don't let the task overwhelm you since you will probably have many different kinds of jobs in several different fields over your work lifetime. However, you have to start somewhere.

If you have many different areas of interest, take a sheet of paper and label one half "pros" and the other "cons." Then, write down your top three areas of interest and list the pros and cons below them.

Among the factors to consider for each subject area are: (1) your interest/passion in the subject area, (2) how it will benefit society,

(3) the likelihood of your being able to graduate in that field and find a job to your liking and (4) the amount of money and security a job in that field offers.

Here's a word about job security. The work world is constantly undergoing tremendous change. Some companies merge and come together, others reduce their workforce periodically to save money and some go bankrupt as they are unable to meet business challenges.

Your best job security is to always be learning and expanding your knowledge and skills. You may also have an entrepreneurial bent so your initial jobs may turn out to be learning experiences for the time you open your own business.

One way to determine your field of interest is to see it in action and talk to the people working in the field. For example, if you want to be a software programmer, call up software companies and make appointments to talk to or visit in person with programmers. Speak to people who have been working in the field two years, five years and ten years. See what their perspective is on the work, their enjoyment of it and whether they'd recommend that you enter the field in view of your interests and abilities and *their* experiences.

Every six months during the high school years (and yearly throughout your work career), repeat this process of listing your career choices, writing down the pros and cons and conducting your real-world interviews.

2. Get college counseling and info on colleges

Just as you should start to determine your field of interest as soon as you enter high school, at the same time you should start thinking about the type of college you'd like to attend.

Start by talking with a college counselor. Review your list of fields of interest and the input you've received from talking to people working in these jobs. Then take the counselor's information and gather your own information through the Internet — three sites to definitely check out are *http://nces.ed.gov/ipeds/cool/*, *www.collegeboard.com* and *www.collegedirectorynetwork.com*. Some states have a wealth of data on their public universities on state board of regents' websites (e.g., in Ohio, look at *http://regents.ohio.gov/colleges_universities.php*).

3. Make a list of colleges
Make your list of colleges with the assistance of a college counselor and your parents. Here's what to look for:

- the reputation of the college especially in your main field of interest
- the reputation of the college in general
- whether it's a small, medium or large college
- how close the college is to your home

Don't use cost as a factor yet. There may be extra financial aid available from more expensive colleges so the cost may not end up being higher (or much higher) than others you are considering.

4. Look at the money issues
Now is the time to look at the money issues and to give your parents a homework assignment — to read this chapter after you finish it.

Discuss money issues with a counselor and your parents. Work with your parents and use the calculators and information at *www.fafsa4caster.ed.gov/*, *www.finaid.org* and *www.collegeboard.com* to help you through the process, including finding ways to pay for college. See Money-Smart Way #50 below on college costs.

5. Keep the long-term picture in mind

You may be looking ahead to graduate school, too. Certain undergraduate colleges can help you get into a graduate program in your particular field of interest.

6. Look at the big picture of life

The process of applying to college can be very stressful. Unfortunately, part of that process is not being accepted everywhere you'd like to be admitted.

Remember this as you go through the application process. You may not get into your "perfect" college. A rejection by a college is *not* a measure of your self-worth and for every door that closes in life, another one opens. Going to a particular college does not guarantee success in life, nor does it prevent it. Above all, you need to be a *great person* in life more than you need to graduate from a *great college.*

49. Community colleges and Early College High Schools

The right college for you may first be a community college (also known as a junior college). Even with the financial aid available at four-year colleges and universities, it may be impossible to match the much lower tuition cost at local colleges.

Generally, community colleges are smaller campuses located closer to your parents' home. You may be able to live at home to further reduce the cost of college. And you may need or want to stay nearby to help work in a family business.

Be realistic about yourself. Not everyone is ready to live apart from parents across the country at age 18 or to deal with the pressures of a major university or college. One-fourth of all college students are enrolled part-time in two-year public colleges.

And many community colleges offer a quality education that can lead to a four-year college or university. Often it's easier to transfer into a four-year school as a junior than to be accepted at the beginning as a freshman.

Also, be on the lookout for creative solutions for more affordable bachelor's degrees. Maricopa Community Colleges in Arizona entered into a partnership with Indiana University where students can earn a bachelor's degree in general studies by taking 90 credits (3 years) at Maricopa colleges and the other 30 credits *online* through Indiana University. That really brings down the cost of a degree.

Also, consider Early College High Schools (*www.earlycolleges.org*) where students at certain small high schools *simultaneously* earn both a high school diploma and either a two-year Associate of Arts degree or enough college credits to enter a four-year, liberal arts program as a junior.

50. Calculating a college-size nest egg

College may be more affordable than you think. But figuring out in advance exactly how much *your* college education will cost isn't easy for three reasons: (1) sticker prices vs. net prices; (2) average net prices vs. your price and (3) how long you'll be in college.

Sticker prices vs. net prices

If you walk into a car dealership to buy a car, you'll see a sticker price (cost) on a car's window or windshield. That's not the price you should pay for the car. Instead, through negotiation, you can get a lower price. Similarly, college tuition costs and fees have a sticker (published) price and a net price. Try not to pay the sticker price here either. Many students pay the sticker price because they are not aware of all the sources and amounts of grants and scholarships available to them that can reduce college costs.

According to the College Board, for the 2006-2007 school year, the *national average sticker (published) price* for just tuition and fees was $2,272 at two-year public colleges; $5,836 at four-year public colleges and universities (for state residents) and $22,218 at four-year *private* colleges and universities. That's just one year's sticker price.

Now look at the net prices. The *national average net price* for tuition and fees for that year was $100 (a $2,200 drop) at two-year public colleges; $2,700 (a $3,100 drop) at four-year public colleges and universities (for state residents) and $13,200 (a $9,000 drop) at four-year *private* colleges and universities. That's quite a difference. As you can see, with sticker prices or net prices, going to a community college or a four-year public college or university can cut your costs considerably. Also see Money-Smart Way #51 for other ways to reduce college costs.

What are net prices? *Net prices* are the sticker prices *less* any grants, scholarships and higher education tax benefits (tax deductions and tax credits). Net prices show the true out-of-pocket costs.

Grants are financial aid, based on need, which you *don't* have to repay. Scholarships are given for special academic, artistic or athletic abilities and *don't* need to be repaid. (By contrast, the other main type of financial aid, loans, does need to be repaid by you.)

Average net prices vs. your price

Since average net prices vary by region, school and tax benefits, your cost might be very different. Also, it's difficult to predict your net price in advance because even within the same college or university, students pay different net prices depending on their family income and resources, eligibility for grant aid, academic qualifications and other factors. However, average net prices and average sticker prices at least give you a range of dollar amounts that you can use as rough guidelines. Here's another statistic that may help you. Over 40% of students in 2006-2007 paid less than $6,000 in *sticker price* tuition and fees and 65% paid less than $9,000 in *sticker price* tuition and fees.

Other costs
Besides tuition and fees, books cost around $1,000 per year as do transportation costs. Room and board costs average around $7,500 per year (living at home can save money here).

How long you'll be in college
Yearly costs really add up so it's important to know for budgeting purposes whether you'll graduate in four years. Keep in mind that, on average, students take 5.3 years to earn a bachelor's degree in private colleges and 6.2 years in public colleges. Extra years in college also mean extra time for education inflation to increase costs.

Calculating the expected family contribution
Most families don't have savings to cover 100% of college costs. However, whatever can be saved will be a big help. In general, the difference between savings and costs can be paid through loans, grants, scholarships or other financial aid, including work-study programs. However, as time goes on, it's getting more difficult to find *enough* sources and *affordable* sources to pay all the college bills.

That's why you'll want to use *FAFSA4caster* (*www.fafsa4caster.ed.gov/*), a great tool launched in 2007 by Federal Student Aid (*www.FederalStudentAid.ed.gov*), an office of the U.S. Department of Education. It provides you and your family with an early estimate of eligibility for federal student aid, the expected family contribution and eligibility for a Pell grant. The tool is based on the *FAFSA* (Free Application for Federal Student Aid), the qualifying form for federal financial aid. You can also do estimated financial aid calculations at *www.finaid.org/calculators/finaidestimate.phtml*.

51. 10 ways to reduce college costs

Here are 10 ways to reduce costs:

1. Take advance placement classes in high school that qualify for college credits.

2. Take courses at a community college while you're in high school (during the summer and possibly during the school year) to get a head start on college credits.

These first two steps can reduce how long you need to pay for a college education, give you a college experience in advance and give you the option to reduce your college workload.

3. Use military service education benefits.

4. Take advantage of nonmilitary service programs such as AmeriCorps (*www.americorps.org*) to obtain college assistance.

5. Get all available grants and scholarships since you don't have to repay them (as compared to loans). Pell Grants are a federal financial aid program based on need.

Scholarship sites

www.collegeanswer.com
www.collegeboard.com
www.fastweb.com
www.finaid.org
www.scholarships.com
http://studentaid.ed.gov (click the *Tools and Resources* tab and
            then click the "Go" button for *Scholarship Search*)

6. Have you or your parents shop around for the best deal on loans. There are Stafford Loans, PLUS loans, Sallie Mae Signature Student Loans, home equity loans and loans against a 401(k) plan. Loans vary

in size, the interest rate, the tax deductibility of interest, the repayment period and how the family income and assets affect the amount available. Try to get federal loans before private loans.

7. As early as possible, use the *FAFSA4caster* at *www.fafsa4caster.ed.gov/* and also become familiar with FAFSA (Free Application for Federal Student Aid at *www.fafsa.ed.gov*), the federal financial aid application. Be sure you meet application deadlines.

8. Make sure your family is aware of the different financial aid results depending on who owns the assets being invested and saved for your college education (see Money-Smart Way #52).

9. Make sure your family is aware of available tax benefits connected with funding a college education (see Money-Smart Way #53).

10. Have your parents negotiate grants, costs and aid with the colleges.

52. Right and wrong ways to save for college costs

Saving money for college is much more than just setting aside a certain amount every month or year. Figuring out the right way to save can be a complex process involving federal and state income tax and gift tax laws as well as financial aid laws and regulations. And these laws and rules may have exceptions or fine print (e.g., *distributions* from a 529 plan set up by a grandparent may be treated differently than a 529 plan set up by a parent).

Since these laws and regulations can change over time, it's important for you and your parents to become (and stay) aware of the rules of the game. (As you read the following pages in this part, you'll better understand another benefit of a college education — it can teach you how to understand technical subjects like the ones you'll find in the work world and the rest of this Part Seven.)

Here are some guidelines to help you figure out how to save for college and qualify for financial aid.

10 key questions

The 10 key questions to ask *before* choosing a college-saving investment vehicle are:

1. Will this form of investment reduce my chances of getting financial aid, scholarships or grants?

2. If so, what would the reduction be?

3. Are there any current income tax benefits from this investment?

4. Are there any future income tax and/or estate tax benefits from this investment?

5. Are there any current gift tax issues?

6. What happens to the funds if I don't go to college?

7. What are the costs and fees of maintaining this investment?

8. Is there a less expensive alternative that would give the same result?

9. Is there a maximum annual amount that can be contributed to this type of investment?

10. Can only certain expenses (e.g., tuition and books but not room and board) be paid for income tax free from this type of investment?

Maximizing your chances of financial aid

Be aware of the name game. Whether savings are put in your name, your parents or your grandparents can affect the amount of financial aid. Also be aware that the rules of the game can change over time.

Advantages of saving under your parents' names

It is usually better for your parents to save in their names, not yours. The reason is that when public universities and colleges decide how much to give out in financial aid, student assets are assessed at a 20% rate each year (as of July 1, 2007) as compared to a 5.64% rate for assets of parents. For some private schools, the rate is 25% for student-owned assets and 5% of parents' assets.

So, if your parents save in their names and not yours, you are more likely to qualify for aid (or at least some aid) than if accounts are in your name due to the 20% vs. 5.64% rate differential.

There's another reason to save in your parents' names rather than yours — some assets (IRAs, 401(k) plans, home equity, annuities and life insurance policies) of parents currently aren't counted in the *federal* needs analysis (note that schools may count home equity). Assets saved in a grandparent's name including 529 plans (see #53 below) generally aren't counted at all when calculating financial aid eligibility. However, it's unclear right now whether distributions from a grandparent-owned 529 plan would affect financial aid eligibility.

Disadvantages of saving under your parents' names

If your parents save in their names, it exposes the college funds to certain risks.

The funds could be spent for other purposes (e.g., a car or a vacation). Your parents' creditors (people your parents owe money to) could get their hands on the funds. Estate (death) tax could be due on the funds if one or both of your parents passed away. The funds could be lost due to a divorce or a death if you are part of a blended family (i.e., a child of a prior marriage). Especially if this is a second marriage for a parent of yours, your college education fund could end up being divided or inherited by your step-parent. It may be wise for your parent(s) who have remarried to have a written agreement to protect your education nest egg.

Saving in your name

An alternative is to save funds in your name. Usually this is done in accounts opened up under the Uniform Transfers to Minors Act ("UTMA") or the Uniform Gifts to Minors Act ("UGMA"). In general, with UTMA or UGMA accounts, your parents or the people they appoint retain control of the money as the manager of the account (as the custodian) until you reach a designated age (usually age 18 or 21).

The main risk of using an UTMA or UGMA account from your parents' point of view is that once you reach the designated age, you can decide how to use the savings without anyone's approval. You might decide not to attend college and use the funds for another purpose. For that reason and the fact that having accounts in your name will hurt your chances of getting financial aid, many parents do not set up these accounts.

Note that it *may* be possible now for financial aid purposes to change a student-owned asset (e.g., an UTMA) into a parent-owned asset (e.g., a 529 plan—see Money-Smart Way #53 below). However, such a change has legal and tax complexities and may not be allowed down the road.

53. Tax-saving ideas and paying for college

The federal government offers many tax benefits to help pay for your college education. Although most of these benefits apply to your parents, some may also apply to you, your grandparents, other relatives and friends. States may offer tax benefits, too. Below are the general rules on seven tax-saving strategies that can help pay for your college education:

1. 529 Plans

There are three types of 529 plans. Two are for public institutions (State College 529 Plans and 529 Prepaid Plans) and one is for private colleges (Independent 529 Plans). 529 plans are also known as Section 529 Plans because the tax rules for these plans are in section 529 of the Internal Revenue Code. Two sites with information on 529 plans are *www.collegesavings.org* and *www.savingforcollege.com*. You can see plan comparison options at *www.collegesavings.org/planComparison.aspx* and *www.independent529plan.org/compare.html*.

Before investing in a plan, find out the fees, costs, refund possibilities, transferability to another family member and federal and state tax implications. Note that there *may* be tax complications if you start with one state's plan and then switch the money to another state's plan.

Advantages of 529 Plans

Generally, 529 plans offer income tax *and* financial aid advantages. Earnings on plan investments grow tax-deferred (no federal income tax is due each year as the investments grow in value) and if the investments are used for permitted educational purposes, the distributions from the investments are federal income tax free.

The earnings may also be free of any state income tax (check your state law, too) and contributions to a 529 plan may be eligible for a state income tax deduction or credit. Some states give a tax deduction even if a contribution is made to the plan of another state. The plan rules differ from state to state so the fine print always needs to be read. If the tax rules aren't followed, there can be federal and state income tax and penalties.

For financial aid purposes, 529 plan investments are *not* counted as student-owned assets. That increases the chances of getting financial aid because 20% of student assets are taken into account each year as compared to 5.64% of parents' countable assets.

State 529 College Savings Plans

With this type of 529 plan, contributions are made by your parents or others on your behalf and depending on the results of the investments (savings accounts, stocks, bonds, etc.), that's how much you'll have on hand to pay for college. There is no guarantee as to how much you'll have with this approach.

State 529 Prepaid Plans

With these prepaid plans, the contributions made now are guaranteed to pay for future tuition costs at today's prices.

Note, however, that this type of plan does *not* guarantee admission to a college or university. It's just a way of locking in and paying for future tuition costs *if* you attend that college or university. Since the risk of a more costly than expected education is on the colleges under this type of plan, some state plans have increased fees over time, increased the prices or halted enrollments.

Independent 529 (I529) Plans

The Independent 529 Plan (I529) is a prepaid plan sponsored by some *private* colleges. Part (or all) of the current tuition cost can be paid now and it is guaranteed that that same percentage (or all) of future tuition cost will be paid off when you enter college. For example, if your parents pay 50% of the current year's tuition, then you are guaranteed to have paid 50% of a future year's tuition cost.

Note that with this type of plan, it's only the undergraduate and other mandatory fees that are covered—not books or room and board (which other 529 plans cover).

2. Gifts

Relatives, especially grandparents, may want to make gifts to pay for your educational costs. There are two main ways your relatives can make gifts to or for you.

First, they can give an unlimited amount directly to the educational institution to pay for tuition without any federal gift tax being due. This can reduce your financial aid benefits.

Second, they can each give you up to $12,000 per calendar year (the limit can change over time) without any federal gift tax being due. Larger gifts would reduce their federal estate tax exclusion. State law may be different.

However, because gifts made directly to you can reduce your chances of receiving college financial aid or possibly be spent by you for noncollege purposes, many relatives are reluctant to make direct gifts. Instead, grandparents may make gifts to your parents since currently only 5.64% of parents' countable assets are looked at for financial aid purposes as compared to 20% of a student's assets.

3. U.S. Savings Bonds

U.S. Savings Series EE bonds and Series I bonds (issued after 1989 in the name of someone over age 23; owned personally and outside of an IRA or retirement plan; and used to pay for your college education) may be an income tax-free source to pay for education. The interest on the bonds is *not* taxable for federal income tax purposes depending on the income of the bond owner in the year the bonds are cashed in.

4. Coverdell ESAs (Education Savings Accounts)

Coverdell ESAs, formerly known as Education IRAs, allow yearly contributions up to $2,000 — this can continue through your 18th birthday. Everyone's contributions together (parents, grandparents, etc.) cannot exceed the $2,000 yearly total. The earnings in a Coverdell ESA grow income tax free. Withdrawals are *not* subject to federal income tax or penalties when used for certain college-related purposes.

5. Hope and Lifetime Learning Tax Credits for Education

The cost of your college education may be reduced by taking advantage of special tax breaks known as the Hope and Lifetime Learning Tax Credits.

6. IRAs

Withdrawals can be made in some cases from traditional IRAs and Roth IRAs to pay for certain education costs. Although subject to income tax, withdrawals should avoid early withdrawal penalties.

7. Tax-deductible interest

Student-loan interest and home equity interest may be tax deductible.

54. Repaying college debt

Just about every college student needs to take out student loans to pay for college. When you graduate from school, you'll probably have both a diploma and an IOU in hand (hopefully just from student loans and not also from credit card usage).

Once you graduate, be diligent in repaying your college loans on time. The better you are at repaying your loans, the better your credit rating will be (see Money-Smart Way #31). This will help you get loans in the future and at lower interest rates.

It's your responsibility to repay your loans on time. If you move or if your loan has been transferred to another lender, you may not receive a billing statement on time. Don't wait for a lender to find you. Locate your lenders and find out the due dates and required payments by contacting the National Student Loan Data System (*www.nslds.ed.gov*).

With some loan programs, the lender may reduce future interest charges if you make the initial payments (e.g., the first four years of payments) on time. You may also receive a lower interest rate from the beginning if loan payments are automatically made from your checking or savings account.

It may pay to consolidate (combine) several federal college loans into one loan to lock in a *fixed rate* and make it simpler to keep track of debts and payments. You cannot consolidate private loans into the federal consolidation loan program. Generally, keep federal college loans and private student loans separate to get a lower interest rate and to retain the more flexible repayment and forgiveness provisions on federal loans.

If you return to school for at least half time, you may be able to defer (delay) payments on your loan. Ask. If you have a 10-year public college or university student loan and you need to make smaller repayments each month, your lender may let you make payments over a 30-year period. Again, ask. Visit *www.salliemae.com* or call the Federal Student Aid Center (800/4-FED-AID) for additional information on different repayment options that may work for you.

On the other hand, it may be your parents who are repaying their own home equity loan that was used to pay for your education. The risk there is that a default could cause a home foreclosure.

PART EIGHT
Money-Smart Ways to Bank

55. Checking accounts

A checking account is an account with a bank or other financial institution that is used to pay for your purchases or other bills. You may prefer an *online checking account* (see Money-Smart Way #59).

If you just want to save your money and not write checks, instead use a savings account or other investment to help your savings grow. (To keep it simpler, Part Eight will use the term "banks" to represent the more cumbersome phrase "banks and other financial institutions.")

Another type of account, a *money market account*, is a type of savings account that allows you to write a limited number of checks each month or each quarter. If your check writing needs are very limited, you may want to have a money market account instead of a checking account.

Opening a checking account

When you open a checking account, the first step is for you to put some money in the account as the initial deposit.

See Money-Smart Way #59 for more information on *online checking accounts* and Money-Smart Way #60 regarding insured accounts.

Do's and don'ts in selecting your checks

As part of opening an account, the bank then has checks prepared that show your name and address (and possibly your phone number).

To keep your privacy, think about getting checks that only have your first initial and your full last name rather than your full first and last names. For a similar reason, you may want to get checks without your address or at least without your phone number.

There are different check styles. Some checks have tear-off end stubs with the check number that let you write down the date of the check, the amount and the payee (the recipient of the check). This can be a handy way to go so you don't have to carry around your checkbook register (see below) everywhere you go.

Using your checking account

Over time you will put additional money into the account by making deposits.

Then as you write checks to pay for your purchases or other bills, those amounts will be deducted from your account. There may also be regular fees and special fees deducted by the bank for having a checking account (see Money-Smart Way #56 for more information).

Managing a checking account develops skills you will use throughout your life including:

- learning how to pay bills on time

- determining which purchases you can afford to make now or in the future

- keeping track of your money in the checking account (also known as balancing your checkbook — see Money-Smart Way #57 for tips on this)

Don't bounce your checks

If you don't have the money in your account to pay for a check you've written, there can be many problems. The least of your problems will be that the bank will charge you a fee for the returned ("bounced") check (also known as a "rubber check" since it bounces right back to you without payment going through). The merchant you tried to pay may charge you a fee, too.

Bounced checks can affect your credit rating, too (see Money-Smart Way #31). There can also be more serious problems caused by bounced checks including claims that you were trying to defraud a merchant.

56. How to select a checking account

Checking accounts are not the same at every bank. Even within a bank, there may be many different types of checking accounts available to you.

To select the right checking account for you, do some comparison shopping. Since this type of shopping has a lot of details, you'll want to make a chart to record these details, which are listed below, call different banks and write down the answers. Then compare the information to make a decision on where to open an account.

Seven key issues

1. What checking account fees are charged?

Ask for a list of the fees charged on a checking account. Fees may include:

- a monthly fee (even a no-fee account may impose a charge if the balance falls below a certain dollar amount)

- a handling fee for processing each check

- a fee for using tellers rather than an ATM for deposits and withdrawals

- a check-bouncing fee if the dollar amount of your checks is larger than the amount of your funds in the account

- a fee for getting the actual cancelled (paid) checks back each month with your monthly statement (the return of physical checks is being phased out)

- a fee for receiving just digital copies of your checks with your monthly statement

- check printing fees (sometimes you will be given a certain number of free checks when you open an account)

2. What are the ATM fees?

Find out what fees, if any, are charged when:

- you use an ATM from your bank

- you use an ATM from another bank

  You could end up paying no fees, one fee or two fees: (1) an ATM fee and (2) an access fee if the machine is part of another bank's system. If you want to avoid paying another bank's access fee, open an account at a bank with more ATM locations or with free access to more ATMs. (See Money-Smart Way #58 for more information on ATMs.)

3. How much are the online banking fees?

Online banking may be free. Find out if there are fees for banking over the Net.

4. Is interest paid on personal checking accounts?

Checking accounts often do not pay interest. If interest is paid, it is usually much less than the interest rate paid on savings accounts or money market accounts.

5. Is overdraft protection available?

If you qualify for "overdraft protection," banks will honor (pay for) checks you've written above the current balance in your account up to the overdraft amount.

The "over" of overdraft refers to the bank covering (paying) checks that are over the balance in your account. This can be valuable protection for you since it can help you avoid accidentally writing a bounced check. Find out the cost of using this protection. Don't rely on overdraft protection on a regular basis. Look at it as emergency backup protection to help protect your credit history.

6. Where are the bank branches/ATMs located?

If you will be doing your banking in person (as compared to doing it over the phone, through the mail or over the Internet), find a bank that's convenient for you.

7. Are there any special deals now?

It never hurts to ask. You may receive a certain number of free checks or a lower or no monthly fee.

57. Balancing your checkbook

Balancing your checkbook helps you know how much money is really in your checking account at all times. Knowing your balance will help you avoid writing checks that can bounce and affect your credit rating.

What does balancing a checkbook really mean?

When you balance a checkbook, you match up your records with the bank's on your checking account.

If you are balancing your statement via online banking, you use similar steps to the ones shown below to get in balance except that by typing in the amounts online, the bank site does the arithmetic for you and helps automate the balancing process.

For non-online accounts, your bank will give you a small booklet, known as a *checkbook register* (sometimes called a *checkbook*). In your checkbook register, write down all of your checks, ATM withdrawals, electronic withdrawals, automatic payments, deposits and bank fees as they occur in chronological (date) order, adding and subtracting as needed. If you do this simple math and recordkeeping as you go in your checkbook register, you will know how much money you have in your account at any time.

Balancing your checkbook is the process of comparing your records as of today to a bank statement that shows how much was in your account at an earlier date (for example, the last day of the prior month).

Your checkbook balance

If you write down every transaction (check, deposit, etc.) in your checkbook register, you can have an up-to-date total of what's in your account on any given day. That total is known as your *checkbook balance*. Write down that total in pencil since your math may be off.

Total up your checkbook balance about every 10 days (rather than once a month) so you have a good idea of how much is in your account at any given time.

The bank balance

On the bank statement sent to you, the bank has its own calculation of your latest balance (called the *bank balance* or other variations such as *The Statement Ending Balance*).

Putting the two in sync is balancing your checkbook

Although your checkbook should show every transaction that affects your account, your bank statement will have a time lag and not include transactions such as checks you've written and recorded but haven't been processed yet by the bank. Look at the "ending date" on your bank statement to see where your bank's information stops on the statement.

You need to compare your checkbook balance dollar amount with the bank balance and bring them in sync to see if you've overlooked pluses or minuses to your account.

As just mentioned, the bank statement sent to you won't list checks that haven't been cashed as of the bank statement's ending date. The bank doesn't know about these checks as of the statement ending date. There may also be deposits you made after the ending date on the bank statement that don't appear on the bank's statement.

The steps to balance your checkbook

Note that you may only need to do the first six steps to get your checkbook in balance. The last two steps are to help you handle problems that may come up in the balancing process.

Step One

Get your checkbook balance up to date. Write down in your checkbook register any bank fees listed on the statement . Go through your checkbook register with a calculator (or using your cellphone's calculator or your computer's) and write down in the checkbook register, in pencil, the current balance in your account.

Step Two

Locate banking transactions (checks, deposits, etc.) that weren't listed on the current bank statement or any prior bank statement. Uncashed checks are known as *outstanding checks*. The "*out*standing" part does not mean that the checks have any special merit — they're just *out* there, uncashed, as of the time the bank statement was prepared.

Sometimes, checks will be uncashed for months. It's important to be aware of these outstanding checks. You don't want to bounce a check because you relied on the last ending balance on a bank statement to show how much money you have on hand. If that old, outstanding check finally gets cashed after the last statement, you may run short of funds if you haven't already deducted outstanding checks as money already spent. Remember, with non-online banking, the ending bank balance does not get reduced for uncashed checks.

Put the checks returned with the statement in numerical order with the lowest number first. Go through your checkbook register and put a checkmark next to the amount of each cashed check that you have in hand.

Circle the amounts of uncashed outstanding checks that haven't been returned to you. The bank statement doesn't show the outstanding checks because they weren't cashed as of the ending date on the bank statement.

Look for any ATM withdrawals, electronic withdrawals, automatic payments and bank fees and make sure they're written down in your checkbook register.

Compare the deposits on the statement with the ones in your checkbook register. Put a checkmark in your register for deposits shown on the bank statement. Circle the deposits that are not shown on the statement.

Step Three

On the back of the bank statement or on a separate piece of paper, write down what the bank shows as the ending balance on the statement.

Step Four

On that same paper, write down the date and amount of all deposits and other credits (pluses for you) that don't appear on the bank's statement.

Step Five

Add Step Three plus Step Four to come up with a subtotal.

Step Six

On that same paper, list all of the checks you've written and other debits (minuses) that *don't show up* on the statement. Total up all of these items on your calculator and subtract them from the dollar amount in Step Five.

This dollar amount should match the dollar amount in your checkbook register. If it doesn't, then your checkbook register and bank statement are not in balance. Don't worry. The good news is that you can solve every checking account balancing mystery. Eventually, all the numbers will add up correctly. Steps Seven and Eight tell you how to do it.

Step Seven

First, see whether the bank statement shows that you have more or less than you think you do. That will help you determine whether you should be expecting to find a deposit you didn't write down, a fee or charge that you've overlooked or a deposit or check written down with the wrong amount.

Now you need to be a detective to find out why you're out of balance. If you see the dollar difference is $9, there's a good chance you reversed the digits (e.g., writing down $21 as $12) when writing down a check or a deposit.

Look at the checking statement to see if there are bank fees or automatic payments from your account that you haven't written down in your checkbook register.

If you haven't found the difference yet, see if there is still an unpaid outstanding check from an earlier statement that you forgot to list in Step Six.

There are three other items to check. Sometimes a check is not returned to you (so it looks like an outstanding check) but it has been cashed and is listed in numerical order on the bank statement or in a withdrawal section of the bank statement. See if there are checks like this that you've listed as outstanding checks.

Then, if you're still out of balance, take a look at the dollar amounts of each check and deposit shown on the statement and compare them to what you've written down in your checkbook register.

Finally, double-check all of the fees, charges and automatic payments to make sure they're listed in your checkbook register and use your calculator to check your math.

Step Eight

Once your checkbook register is in balance with the bank's ending balance, write your checkbook register balance in ink. This will help make this balanced amount stand out.

Right above that total put this notation "Bal OK" (balance OK) and put in the ending date (the month/day/year) of the statement you balanced to (e.g., 12/31/08) next to that. This way, next month, you'll know your checkbook was balanced as of the December 31, 2008 statement.

Now, go one step further. For any outstanding checks, right below "Bal OK 12/31/08" for example, write O.S. (for outstanding checks) and list the check numbers of the outstanding checks. When you go to balance next month's statement, this can be a quick way of locating outstanding checks from prior months.

Sometimes checks don't get cashed for many months and it can be time-consuming to go back through months of your checkbook register to locate the outstanding checks. This short notation provides a quick way for you to look through your checkbook register to locate those older checks that weren't cashed as of the last statement and need to be listed as outstanding checks in Step Six.

58. ATMs

ATMs or automated teller machines grew out of the idea in the 1970s of having a vending machine for money.

ATMs can be very convenient but you need to find out about any charges for using the machine, whether it's an ATM of your bank or another bank.

Beyond the issue of fees, using ATMs requires some safety precautions on your part:

1. ATMs use your PIN (personal identification number) to identify you. Memorize your number. Don't carry the number on you. If you lose a paper with the number, someone might access your account.

Use a unique PIN for your account. Don't use the same PIN for different bank accounts. Don't use the PIN as your email password or for other sensitive accounts.

2. To help protect your account, take your ATM receipts with you when you leave the machine.

3. Keep your ATM transactions private. Ask people to please move back if they are too close to you and can see what you're doing.

4. Don't use just any ATM. At night, only use ATMs that have good lighting and safe conditions or just wait until the next day.

59. Online banking

Virtually every bank allows you to bank online. What this means is that via the Internet you can pay certain bills electronically, move your money among different accounts and check your balance.

To bank online, you either need to use the bank's software with your computer (or mobile device) or access your account through the Internet. Find out what's free and what costs with online banking and whether your mobile device will work with online banking.

Banking online may save you time and money by reducing or eliminating the need for you to write checks (and pay for stamps) to pay bills. However, not all bills can be paid electronically with online banking. In some cases, a merchant or other vendor will not be electronically connected to the bank. In those cases, a check still needs to be written by someone, in this case the bank, to pay a bill.

As a result, you need to allow additional time when bills are paid by checks through online banking. How much time to allow depends on how quickly the bank prepares checks and mails them out.

There are some bills that you may need to pay yourself instead of through online banking. If payment coupons need to be sent along with a check, your bank usually won't have those coupons. So, if your bank sends in its check without a coupon, the payment may not be credited correctly and you may be subject to late fees.

Avoid handling your banking at wireless hotspots and other locations that may not be secure. For more tips on how to secure your computer, mobile device and your online experiences, see if your library has a copy of the softcover or e-book edition of my book, *Teach Your Computer to Dance: Make Your Computer, Mobile Devices and the Internet Perform for You.*

60. Savings accounts

Just as checking accounts have their own purpose (paying bills), savings accounts have a different purpose — saving for short- and long-term goals.

Savings accounts grow through your deposits and the interest paid on your account. As time goes by, interest is paid on the prior interest kept in the account as well as the deposits you've made. This is called *compound interest* and it is one of the ways for you to achieve your goals and financial independence.

Here's an example. Suppose you open an account with $1,000 and the bank credits (pays) your account interest at 5% per year.

After one year, you'd have $1,050. After two years, the balance would be $1,102.50. After around 14 years, the balance would have doubled to $2,000 (all of these dollar amounts are before considering any income tax that might be due on the interest).

Shopping for a savings account

Since savings accounts may serve short- and/or long-term goals, you may need more than one type of savings account to meet your needs.

The main question you need to answer before shopping for an account is when and how often you'll need to tap into the savings account. The reason this is important is that one type of account called a *certificate of deposit* or *CD* usually pays a higher rate of interest the longer you tie up your money in the account. A CD may also have a penalty that reduces the size of your account if you withdraw money before the end of the specified period of time. Some CDs allow early withdrawals without a penalty.

Another type of account, a *money market account*, is a type of savings account that allows you to write a limited number of checks each month or each quarter.

Since shopping for a savings account involves a lot of details, you'll want to make a chart with the questions below, call different banks and write down their answers. Then compare the information to make a decision on where to open an account. You can get much or all of this information on the Net and sometimes special deals are available only by opening the account on the Net.

Five questions to ask about savings accounts

With any kind of checking or savings account, make sure there is *FDIC insurance*. The FDIC – short for the Federal Deposit Insurance Corporation – is an independent agency of the U.S. government. The FDIC protects you against the loss of your funds if an FDIC-insured bank fails. The basic protected amount is $100,000 (the limit can be higher under certain circumstances).

On your FDIC-insured account, here are five questions to ask:

1. What interest rate is paid, how is it compounded and what is the *annual percentage yield (APY)*?

You want a higher APY. This is the apples-to-apples measuring stick you should use to compare interest rates between different institutions.

The more often interest is credited to your account (compounded), the larger your account can become by having more interest paid on your interest. The annual percentage yield tells you how much the interest rate will really be as interest is paid on interest as well as deposits.

2. Is there a penalty for making early withdrawals? How much is it?

Some CDs charge you a penalty if you withdraw some or all of your money before the end of a specified period.

3. Is there a charge for too many withdrawals?

Some accounts may not charge you an early withdrawal penalty but there may be a limit on how many withdrawals you can make per month without being charged a fee.

4. Where are the bank branches located?

Having convenient branches or ATMs may be important unless you plan to bank online or by mail.

5. Do you have any special deals now?

In some cases, there are special offers but you might need to ask to learn about them.

PART NINE
Money-Smart Ways
to Handle Paperwork

61. Starting to pay bills and file tax returns

If you don't already have a checking account, ask your parents to let you write out some or all of the checks for the family bills so you'll have this experience. Not only will this prepare you to handle your own bill paying, it will give you an appreciation of how much it costs to keep a roof over your head with everyone comfortable inside.

Ask to see your parents' income tax returns. Find out how the amount of income tax due can be reduced by certain deductions and credits and how to plan ahead to reduce the income tax bite. Keep in mind that not all parents are comfortable showing their income tax returns to their children.

62. A system for paying your personal bills

There are two kinds of bills: (1) paid bills and (2) unpaid bills that need to be paid.

Your bill paying record is the best indicator of your credit worthiness (see Money-Smart Way #31).

To stay on top of your personal bills (and keep your credit record in good shape), you need a system for paying bills on time. A good system consists of the right tools and the right habits.

The right tools

You need at least two files: (1) a "Paid Bills" file for the current calendar year and (2) an "Unpaid Bills" file.

If you don't have too many bills, it's okay to have just one file for all of your paid bills. Keep the bills organized by calendar year. It's easier to locate bills that way, especially in connection with preparing yearly income tax returns.

Put the latest bill on top. It's easier to file papers that way and they will be in order—reverse chronological (date) order—with the oldest bills at the bottom of the file.

If you pay many different types of bills and need to find a bill quickly, you can set up separate file folders for each type of bill. Once you begin listing (itemizing) expenses for income tax purposes, you may want to have at least two paid bills files: (1) one for tax-deductible items and (2) another file for the rest of your bills.

The key is to set up a file system that works for you and how you'd look to find a bill long after it has been paid.

If you pay every bill by check, you can refer to your checkbook register or online account (both of which should be in chronological order) to see who you paid when.

The only catch with this approach is on credit card purchases. Your checkbook register (or online account) usually only shows the name of the credit card company, not what you purchased or from whom. That being the case, for credit card charges that you'll want to refer back to easily, include a description of the purchase in your checkbook register (or online account), too, when you write the check to the credit card company.

Another reason you may want to refer back to paid bills from time to time is to locate a proof of purchase for a warranty on an item that needs repairing or replacing. Look at Money-Smart Way #29 to see how to set up a warranty file (to keep track of product guarantees) that can be used in connection with a paid bills file.

The right habits

Having the right tools (or file system) is only half the solution. You need the right bill-paying habits, too.

You may have so few bills that you can pay all your bills on the same day (e.g., on the 10th day of the month). If that's the case, you just need to mark your calendar or organizer to pay bills on the 10th.

As time goes on and your life becomes more complicated, you will have bills due on many different dates. That's where the one Unpaid Bills file may not work for you. You may need a 1-31 sorter that has sections for each day of the month. Then, you would file unpaid bills in the sorter far enough in advance of the payment due date for your check to arrive on time. For this system to work, you need to check the sorter every day. Since paying bills on time is important, you may decide to pay some bills early so that you are paying a batch of them at once and having fewer bill-paying days. Then, you could use your calendar or sorter to note, for example, two or three times a month to pay your bills.

One other useful technique is to have a master list of due dates showing when recurring bills should be received (e.g., credit card bills or student loan bills). That way if you don't receive a bill on time, you can contact the creditor to find out the due date and the amount due and write a check on time to avoid any blemish on your credit record.

63. Storing your financial paperwork

Just as you should keep track of your bills on a yearly basis, you should store your financial paperwork with the same system.

Depending on how much paper and how many files you have, you may want to store them in a large, enclosed, heavy-duty folder with a flap and tie known as an expanding wallet.

Always describe the contents on a label affixed to the outside of any folder, wallet or box to help you find any desired information quickly and easily in the future. Besides describing the types of records contained inside (e.g., bank statements, paid bills, etc.), always include the year, too.

If you use file boxes (plastic boxes with lids are good), number the boxes on the outside and prepare a master list itemizing the contents of each box. That will make it easy to find records years down the road.

64. Get a shredder

A cross-cut shredder can keep your documents, personal information and identity more secure.

PART TEN
Money-Smart Ways to Make Your Money Grow

65. Piggy bank riches

Here's a simple, painless way to sock away some money by taking your change each day and putting it in a piggy bank or even a jar. The following example illustrates the financial power of a piggy bank.

Let's assume that starting at age 23, each evening you put that day's loose change in your piggy bank. If, on the average, you feed piggy 50 cents a day and also throw in an extra dollar bill, at the end of every three months, you'd have around $150 to invest. If you put this money in a potentially tax-free retirement plan (a Roth IRA—see Money-Smart Way #80), you could receive it all later on without paying any income tax.

If your contributions average a 10% yearly return (which is the average growth for stocks since 1926), then at age 65, you'd have over $200,000 from your piggy bank. Nice piggy.

66. The big payoff from one decision

Even one-time steps can pay off big. If at age 25 you spend $2,000 less than you planned on a car and invest that $2,000 in a Roth IRA (see Money-Smart Way #80) growing on average 10% per year, you could have almost $100,000 in tax-free dollars at age 65.

67. The trick to saving money

The trick to accumulating money is to make the saving process automatic. "Pay yourself first" from your earnings, gifts or other money received by you. Put a portion of that money into savings.

If you don't grab the savings portion right away, it's human nature for you to run out of money before you can save it. The reason is that saving always ends up at the bottom of your list of what to do with your money. All other expenditures either have a more immediate, short-term benefit or may prove to be more urgent. Instead, you need to make the saving process so automatic you don't need to think about it.

Put a good portion of all the money you receive into a savings account or other investment.

68. Doubling your money: the Rule of 72

There's a quick-and-easy way to *estimate* how long it will take for your money to double in size. You just need to know the Rule of 72. It's a two-step, easy process. Here's how it works.

First, pick the percentage you expect your assets to grow each year. The percentage can be the interest paid to you on a bank account or U.S. Savings Bond or the expected growth in the value of stocks or mutual funds.

Then divide 72 by that yearly percentage. The answer tells you how many years it'll take for your money to double.

Here are two examples. First, if you expect your money to grow at 6% per year, then divide 72 by 6 and the answer is 12. It will take 12 years for your money to double at a 6% per year growth rate.

If instead, you expect a growth rate of 12% per year, then 72 divided by 12 gives an answer of 6 years for your money to double.

Ways to use the Rule of 72

The Rule of 72 can be very useful when you're trying to estimate how much money you'll have in your nest egg in the upcoming years.

Assume you've saved $2,000 and you're age 22. You want to know how long it will take for that $2,000 to double if it increases at 8% per year.

Here's the calculation: 72 divided by 8 equals 9 so it will take 9 years to double. After 9 years, at age 31, you'd have $4,000 (2 times $2,000). If the same 8% growth rate continued, then 9 years later at age 40, you'd have $8,000 (2 times $4,000).

To see the power of compound growth (see Money-Smart Way #69), let's play with this a little longer. Nine years later at age 49, you'd have $16,000. At age 58, you'd have $32,000. At age 64, you'd have $64,000. That's all from a one-time $2,000 investment.

Now see the power of an extra percent or in this case, two percent growth per year. You might not think it makes that big a difference but think again. Every percent counts in growth and in expenses.

If the growth rate were 10% per year instead of 8% per year, then it would take 7.2 years (72 divided by 10) to double your money. Over the same time period as the earlier example, the same $2,000 would grow to $113,000 at a 10% rate (as compared to the $64,000 at an 8% annual rate).

Remember that the Rule of 72 is an estimating tool. As the percentage growth rate goes higher, the answer is less accurate. Here's why. To double your money, you need it to increase by 100%. The Rule of 72 says a 72% return will double your money in one year (72 divided by 72 equals 1). Your biggest problem should be having such a high growth rate that the Rule of 72 doesn't produce an exact answer as to when your money will double. Note that the Rule of 72 does not include the possible impact of income tax (see Money-Smart Way #20).

69. The power of compound growth

You just saw how the Rule of 72 (Money-Smart Way #68) lets you estimate how long it will take for your money to double over time. That doubling doesn't happen by magic.

The power behind the growth is *compound growth* (sometimes called *compound interest*). Banks, insurance companies and money-smart people know how to use compound growth to get results.

Compound growth is the reason why *the earlier* you start saving for college or your financial independence, *the less* you'll have to put away each month to get the same result. With compound growth, once you've worked for your money, your money starts working for you.

Although compound growth is powerful at any age, look at two examples that show the power of long-term compound growth and then read the explanation of why it works.

Scenario One

Starting at age 20, Sally puts $2,000 a year of her salary into a Roth IRA (i.e., a type of retirement account that potentially can be income tax free). At ages 21 and 22, she also adds $2,000 each year from her salary. Then, she stops making any contributions. If those three $2,000 contributions generate a return (or growth rate) of 10% per year, then at age 60 she will have $225,000 — that's $225,000 from three $2,000 contributions!

Scenario Two

Joe waited until age 40 to make his first $2,000 contribution and then he made $2,000 contributions religiously every year for the next 19 years with a 10% per year return just like Sally. Joe, however, would have $114,000, almost 50% less, at age 60.

The results with compound growth

How can 20 contributions of $2,000 produce much less than three contributions of $2,000? The answer is compound growth.

Compound growth or compound interest refers to the effect over time of an investment growing in value and the reinvested growth (the growth is left in and is not taken out) also increasing over time. With a savings account, compound interest lets you receive interest on your interest. The longer you've invested, the greater the opportunity for compound interest or growth. Here's another example of compound growth. If I gave you a penny and agreed to double the value every day (2¢, 4¢, 8¢, etc.), in one month you'd have over $5,000,000.

70. Diversification

You've probably heard the expression "don't put all your eggs in one basket." The equivalent expression in money matters is "don't put all your nest eggs in one basket."

For example, if you only buy one stock, say in a movie company, and that company has a string of movies that don't do well, then the value of your entire investment may go down in value, too.

If instead, you invest in other movie companies as well, you are spreading your eggs but possibly not far enough apart. Why? What if the movie industry as a whole starts to have lower profits due to a new technology or economic hard times in general? Then, all of your movie company stocks might not do well. (I'm not picking on movie companies—I'm just using them as an example.)

So, ideally, you want stock investments to be spread among many different types of companies and industries. Then if one part of the economy goes bad, only part of your investments hopefully will suffer.

This spreading of the risk among different investments is called *diversification*. Diversification means more than investing in different types of stocks. It includes making different types of investments (including bonds, savings accounts and other forms of investment).

Another way of looking at diversification is by comparing it to your daily meals. Cereal might be great for breakfast but would you want to only eat cereal for breakfast, lunch and dinner, day after day, month after month and year after year? At some point you'd get sick of cereal just like investors might lose their taste for the one and only stock you invested in if you didn't diversify.

Some people diversify their investments by investing in mutual funds. Mutual funds are where you pool your money with other people and professional money managers invest the money.
Even if you invest in many different mutual funds, you may not be diversifying your money. Several of your mutual funds may be investing in the same companies or same types of companies. Many stock brokerage and financial advice websites can analyze the diversification of your investments.

71. What's risky about risk?

You probably know the expression "There's no such thing as a free lunch." What it means is that you don't receive something for nothing.

Along the same lines, you shouldn't expect a bigger profit from one type of investment unless there is more risk to go along with the profit potential.

In fact, that's how the world works. With a riskier investment, investors demand higher profits (or the potential for higher profits).

Find the right risk level for you. You can't avoid all risk so take it on with your eyes wide open. Fortunately, you are young enough to probably bounce back from almost any investment that goes sour. But why go through that experience and trauma!

Five guidelines on risk and investments

1. Every investment has some kind of risk. Determine the risk that goes with each of your investments.

2. If an investment sounds too good to be true, it probably isn't true.

3. If someone promises you a big profit with little or no risk, they probably aren't telling you the whole story.

4. Consider the source when you receive advice about where to invest or put your money.

5. Be careful lending money to friends or relatives or borrowing money from them. It can ruin relationships if there is a problem in repaying the loan or paying it back on time.

72. What inflation costs you

As time goes by, it costs more to live. What costs $100 today will in time cost $200 (or more). You've seen how college tuition rates keep increasing.

A cost of living increase is known as *inflation* or the *inflation rate*. The inflation rate changes every year. Some years it is very high and other years it is low. (It can even be a negative number though that is very rare.) Over the last 40 years, inflation has averaged about 3% per year.

How inflation impacts your future financial security

Your investments have to earn or grow at no less than the inflation rate just for you to stay where you are. If they earn any less, you are worse off.

Here's an example. Suppose it costs $14 to see a movie at a movie theatre (in time, it will cost at least $14 to see a movie due to inflation). If you have $100 to spend over the summer, you can see 7 movies (7 times $14 = $98) and have $2 left over.

If next year's inflation causes movie prices to go up by 10% (i.e., cost an extra $1.40), then you need to have 10% more (or $107.80 total) to still be able to see 7 movies at a $15.40 per movie cost. If you still have $100 (and not $107.80) to spend next summer on movies, then you'll only be able to see 6 movies due to inflation (6 times $15.40 = $92.40).

To know how your investments are doing, you need to know how much your investments are earning or growing *above* the inflation rate. If your investments grow by 10% next year and the inflation rate that year is 4%, then your real rate of return (your profit or progress) is the difference or 6% (10% earnings/growth rate less 4% inflation rate). The difference, 6%, is how much better off you are after subtracting any increase in the cost of living (i.e., the inflation rate).

What inflation costs you

Inflation gets expensive. Just as inflation affects what you can buy, inflation can eat up the value of your investments over time. Even what appear to be small amounts of inflation can add up to a big impact on you over time.

Remember the Rule of 72 back in Money-Smart Way #68. You can use that rule to see the impact of inflation upon your financial well-being.

This rule can not only tell you how long it will take for your investments to double in value, it can tell you how long it will take for inflation to double your costs.

Just divide 72 by the yearly inflation rate and the answer tells you how long it will take for prices to double.

If inflation is 3% per year, in 24 years (72 divided by 3) what costs $10 today will cost $20 then. If inflation is 5% per year, in just 14.4 years (72 divided by 5) what costs $10 today will cost $20 then.

Three inflation lessons to learn

1. It will cost more to live as time goes on.

2. Always calculate how much better off you are by subtracting out the current year's inflation rate from the growth or earnings of your investments.

3. Make sure your investments grow at a higher rate than inflation to keep from falling behind.

73. Getting the right profit on investments

Over the last 80 years, stocks have *averaged* a compounded annual return of around 10%. (Remember compound growth from Money-Smart Way #69.) During the same period, long-term interest rates and bonds have averaged about half of that. All of these rates of return are before taking inflation into account.

Within any given year as well as any 10-year period, each of these types of investments has often suffered tremendous losses as well as enjoyed startling gains. Know that every year will produce different results. Interest rates go up and down all the time. Stock prices change minute by minute.

What average rates of return don't tell you

It's helpful to know average rates of return. What is very important to know is that averages don't tell you the full story. Imagine a stock goes from $100 to $200 in a year's time. Then, during the next year, it drops back down to $140 by year's end.

The average compounded annual rate of return for the two years was around 18% (if you invested $100 at the beginning, you would have had an average increase of 18% per year, resulting in a value of $140 at the end of year two).

However, if you first invested after year 1 when the stock was at $200, your rate of return for year 2 was a negative 30% (a $60 drop from

$200 to $140). That's why you want to see the returns for *each year* in addition to the returns over a period of time to see how volatile (changeable) the rate of return is on an investment.

The value of your money

It's not just stocks, bonds and real estate that change in value over time. The value of everything, even money, changes all the time. An American dollar buys a different amount of European euros, Japanese yen or English pounds at any given moment.

Balancing the investment factors

Also remember, as discussed in Money-Smart Way #71, that the potential of higher returns means taking on more risk. Recall from Money-Smart Way #72 that you need to match the inflation rate, too, just to stay even.

Finding the right profit for you is a personal matter and it depends on many factors including: (1) how soon you need to turn your investment into cash (i.e., to buy a car, pay college tuition, buy a home or open your own business); (2) how comfortable you are in taking on more risk; and (3) how you diversify (divide up) your investments.

74. Investing without using real money

One of the best ways to learn about investing is not to invest with real money. Instead, pretend you have a pot of money (say $25,000) and plan out how you'd invest it.

After you have reviewed alternative investment choices, cut up a piece of paper and on each piece write down the dollar amount and each type of investment you'd like to make.

Then, put the papers under your pillow and see how you sleep the next week. If you're a nervous wreck from make-believe stock market investments, just imagine how the real thing will affect you.

This exercise will teach you something about your tolerance for risk (see also Money-Smart Way #71).

75. Stocks, mutual funds and indexes

When you buy a stock, you own part of a company. Depending on how well or poorly the company is doing, stock in that company can go up or down in value. While one company's stock is going up in value, at the same time stock in other companies could be falling.

Whenever you buy a stock or make an investment, understand why you think it's a good investment.

You may need professional advice to help you make investments. One way you may get professional advice and spread (diversify) your money among many investments at the same time is to invest in a mutual fund.

Mutual funds are companies with professional money managers that pool your money with that of other investors to buy stocks, bonds and other assets. Mutual funds may invest in a limited number of companies or thousands of companies. Before you invest in a mutual fund, look at the fund's performance over time, how diversified its investments are, its costs to you (expenses, fees and loads) and the tax impact of investing in the fund.

Some mutual funds invest in indexes. An index tracks the performance of a particular group of stocks such as the *DJIA* (the *Dow Jones Industrial Average* has the stocks of 30 major companies from a variety of industries), the *S&P 500* (Standard & Poor's 500 Index has

500 leading companies chosen to represent the U.S. economy) and the *Dow Jones Wilshire 5000 Composite Index* (this broad measure of the U.S. stock market tracks the stocks of virtually every publicly traded company). Consider investing some of your money in a broad-based index with low fees.

76. How to read stock prices

Stocks are pieces of ownership in a company. Stocks are bought and sold in different places known as stock exchanges. The main stock exchanges in the United States are the New York Stock Exchange and NASDAQ.

You can buy and sell stocks through a stockbroker or in some cases, directly from companies.

Stocks go up and down in value as prospects change for a company and the economy as a whole. Stocks may change in value constantly during any given day. Newspapers in the financial section publish the prior day's ending stock value and the amount of change from the prior day's ending value. You can also easily see more current stock prices online at financial and news websites.

The stock pages in a newspaper or other financial publication (on or off of the Internet) list more than just what happened to a stock's value the prior day. Usually, they try to give you perspective, a big view, by including:

- the high and low value for a stock during the prior 52 weeks

- how much change in the stock's value has occurred since the most recent January 1 or when the stock first was sold, whichever is the more recent

- information about the *dividends* (payments to stockholders)

- the *price-earnings ratio* (this shows how a company's stock price compares to the company's earnings — generally the lower the number, the less risky the investment; many investors have almost ignored this ratio, especially with Internet-related stocks)

- the high and low value of a stock on the prior day

- the amount of change in a stock's value since the prior day

- the volume or number of shares of a particular company that were traded that day

If you're looking at a stock online, you can quickly call up charts on your screen for different periods of time to see how the stock's price has done over the last three months, six months, one year or longer.

77. How to read the mutual fund pages

Mutual fund pages may show similar information as the stock pages.

Sometimes mutual funds are listed alphabetically and other times by the group or category they belong to based on certain criteria.

Performance results are usually shown for several time periods including the amount of change in a fund's value during the prior day and sometimes the results for the most recent quarter of the year, the year-to-date and the last three years. Other information such as a fund's expenses and charges are sometimes listed, too.

For more information on particular funds, look to newspapers, financial magazines, financial institutions and mutual fund rating services. These days you're more likely to look for this information on the Internet rather than in newspapers.

78. Expenses and taxes

When you make investments, very often there are costs that are charged in making or keeping the investments.

There are two main types of expenses: (1) fees for purchases or sales and (2) other yearly expenses. Taxes are also a consideration.

Fees and expenses

When you buy a stock through a stockbroker, you are charged a fee. Shop around, including the Internet, to see the range of fees. But don't stop there. In some cases, you can also get financial advice from the stock brokerage company. Brokerage firms that give advice might charge extra (or provide it for free). See what you need and pay the right price for you.

Similarly, mutual funds charge fees, too. Some charge fees when you buy into them and others when you take distributions from them. These types of funds are known as *load funds*. There are other funds known as *no-load funds* that do not have this sale/purchase fee.

In addition, there are also annual expenses charged by mutual funds. Compare these annual costs of owning different mutual funds before putting your money into them. Even a 1% yearly difference in fees can really cost you a lot over the years.

Taxes

Mutual funds buy and sell stocks and bonds all the time. Even though you may *reinvest* (keep your money in there and not take any distributions out), you share in any gain each year from a mutual fund equal to your share of the overall fund. This gain is taxable income to you for that year (unless the fund is part of a retirement account that delays or eliminates any income tax on the gain).

Some funds are designed to produce less taxable income to you by purchasing, holding or selling the stocks owned by them with an eye towards reducing any income tax for the investors. These funds are known as "tax efficient" mutual funds.

Speaking of taxes, be aware that mutual funds distribute their gains to their investors before the end of each year. Before you buy a fund, find out *when* they distribute those gains. Otherwise, you might buy into a fund and then have an instant income tax bill for gains that occurred before you became an owner.

79. Savings bonds

U.S. Savings Bonds have some special features.

Because the U.S. government is repaying you, you know you will receive the expected amount when a bond matures (comes due).

In some cases, certain Series EE and Series I savings bonds may be cashed in with no federal income tax due on the interest on the bonds (see Money-Smart Way #53).

U.S. Savings Bonds have traditionally produced interest at a lower rate than the growth rate of stocks. So you may want to diversify your investments. In other words, bonds can be a part of your investments but you'll probably want to consider stocks and mutual funds, too.

As to how much to put into bonds as compared to stocks and mutual funds, take another look at the discussion of risk (Money-Smart Way #71). Remember, in any given year or any given decade, there can be great results or poor results for any investment.

The biggest risk with bonds is inflation.

If you buy a bond, it's an IOU to repay you at some future date and to pay you interest in the meantime. If the interest on the bond is at a fixed rate (e.g., 6%), that doesn't change over time.

If you are to receive 6% interest while inflation (the cost of living) is at 3%, you are making a real return of 3% (6% interest less 3% inflation). If inflation heats up to 7%, then you are really worse off because the cost of living is going up more than the interest you are receiving.

Another type of U.S. Savings Bond (known as the "I" bond) increases the interest rate if inflation goes up. This bond has inflation features built in to help your investment keep up with changes in the cost of living.

80. The ABCs of IRAs

There are two main kinds of IRAs (individual retirement accounts): (1) the *traditional IRA* and (2) the *Roth IRA*. Each year you may be able to contribute some or all of your *earned income* (e.g., wages or salary) to an IRA.

The maximum contribution can change over time (e.g., $4,000 in 2007 and $5,000 in 2008 for someone your age). The dollar amount is a *combined limit* for both types of IRAs. So, whether you're working part-time, full-time, at a summer job or have your own business, look into opening up an IRA.

There are advantages and disadvantages to each type of IRA.

Traditional IRAs

With a traditional IRA, you generally put money in that has *not* been subject to income tax. While your money stays in the IRA, no income tax is paid on the growth or earnings. Depending on your overall tax situation, income tax can be due when the money comes out. The federal tax rate can change over time. It ranged from 10% to 35% in 2007. State income tax may be due, too.

This IRA is a type of *tax-deferred investment* — payment of income tax is delayed during the growing years and is due on distributions.

With a traditional IRA, you *may* qualify to take an income tax deduction for your IRA contributions and save on your current income tax.

Roth IRAs

With a Roth IRA, you put in money that has *already* been subject to income tax. Just as with a traditional IRA, no income tax is paid on the earnings or growth while your money stays in the IRA. Unlike the traditional IRA, a Roth IRA may allow you to receive the distributions free of any income tax.

There is *no* income tax deduction for contributions to a Roth IRA. At your age and income level, the Roth IRA's potential income-tax-free distributions may substantially outweigh the deduction for income tax purposes on contributions available with a traditional IRA. Also, if you have a traditional IRA, you may be able to convert it into a Roth IRA (there are income tax rules and consequences to check out before converting).

Both IRAs are long-term investments

Look at both types of IRAs as a place to put money away for the long term. Generally, withdrawals before age 59½ (and, also, where a Roth IRA has been in effect for less than 5 years) may be subject to income tax and penalties. However, there are some exceptions.

Since there are many rules for each type of IRA (and the rules may change over time), always get advice before making a contribution or a withdrawal.

81. Income tax basics

There's more to accumulating wealth than just saving and investing. What may be just as important is how much of your nest egg you get to keep *after* the payment of income taxes. If you learn how to put a muzzle on the income tax bite by knowing how to minimize taxes, your nest egg can end up considerably larger in the long run.

The four key income tax strategies to reduce the income tax bite are (1) eliminating income tax, (2) delaying income tax, (3) minimizing income tax and (4) reducing income tax with deductions.

Eliminating income tax

With combined federal, state and local income tax rates sometimes approaching 50%, it's a big deal to get tax-free money. Here are two of the ways. First, the earnings and growth as well as your contributions to a Roth IRA *may* be distributed to you free of income tax (see Money-Smart Way #80). And, on the sale of a principal residence, up to $500,000 of profit on the sale *may* be received free of federal (and maybe state) income tax if all the tax requirements are satisfied — within certain limits, this tax benefit can be used repeatedly over time.

Delaying income tax

A great way for your savings and investments to grow over time is to (legally) delay paying income tax on the gains and growth of your assets. That means the growth and gains aren't reduced by income taxes each year during the growing years. This way you'll have a bigger pot of assets that can keep increasing in value year after year. Some investment vehicles, such as a traditional IRA or a 401(k) plan, let your assets grow *tax deferred*. That means that income tax is not paid until distributions are taken.

However, timing isn't everything when it comes to taxes. Tax rates matter, too.

Minimizing income tax rates

There are two main income tax rates: *ordinary income* and *long-term capital gains* tax rates. Ordinary income tax applies to income like your wages and interest. It also applies to withdrawals from traditional IRAs (the tax-deferred IRA). Ordinary income tax is the higher income tax rate (10% to 35% for federal income tax in 2007).

Long-term capital gains tax applies to profits when certain investments (e.g., stocks, bonds and mutual funds) owned by you personally (and not in an IRA or other retirement plan) are sold for a profit after you own them for a minimum period of time (e.g., more than one year). The long-term federal capital gains tax is lower than the ordinary income tax rate—it's generally 5% to 15% in 2007 and it will go down to 0% in some cases starting in 2008.

Reducing income tax with deductions

Another way to accumulate wealth is to utilize tax deductions that reduce your income tax bill. Interest on a home mortgage is one example of a tax deduction. Remember, though, you won't ever be in the 100% income tax bracket. That means that although a tax deduction may save you some money, spending more you can afford will cost you—even with the benefit of a deduction.

82. Owning assets outside of IRAs

You may choose to own assets outside of an IRA or a 401(k) plan. How you own assets can affect when income tax is due and how much will be due. If you buy and sell assets *outside of* an IRA or 401(k) plan, any gains may be subject to income tax in the year of sale. By contrast, gains on assets *owned* in an IRA or 401(k) are not subject to income in the year of sale. The tax bite (except for a tax-free Roth IRA) comes later, when distribution occurs. That's why IRA and 401(k) investments may grow larger over time than personally owned assets. However, if you'll need to access your money in the not too distant future (e.g., to buy a home), money taken out an IRA or 401(k) before normal retirement age may incur tax *and* an early distribution penalty.

Distributions from both traditional IRAs and 401(k) plans are generally subject to the higher ordinary income tax rates. By contrast, gains on sales of personally owned, non-retirement assets may qualify for the lower long-term capital gains tax rate. As you can see, taxes, gains and distributions are complicated.

Determining when you'll need the money can help you find the right way to own investments—inside or outside of an IRA or 401(k) plan.

83. Other types of investments

There are many other types of investments beyond stocks, bonds and savings accounts including real estate, businesses, annuities, IRAs, retirement plans and certain life insurance policies.

For whatever investment you make, understand why you are making the investment and how you can benefit from or lose your investment. Most investments take time to produce a profit. And remember that investments can go down in value, too.

Although some investments may turn a quick profit for you, you may need to stay with your investments for the long haul to make a profit or avoid a loss. One reason is that for certain types of investments, it may not be that easy to sell them and change them into cash (e.g., real estate) and the market may not be very favorable when you first want to sell.

Become knowledgeable about owning real estate since it can both produce income (if all property-related expenses are met) and grow in value over time. Remember, however, that all investments go in cycles. There are periods of upward trends in value and other periods where values go down.

84. An essential 10-step financial checklist

Review this checklist now and periodically down the financial road:

1. Determine your short-term and long-term financial goals and objectives. For example, how important is it for you to own a car or home now or in the near future as compared to your other goals? Since there is never enough money to satisfy all your needs and desires, you need to know what's most important to you now and in the long run.

2. Start saving as soon as possible.

3. Diversify investments (don't put all of your nest eggs in the same basket).

4. Take the time and effort to keep track of how your investments are doing (even if you have a financial advisor).

5. Consider the effect of inflation.

6. Assess your risk comfort level before you make an investment.

7. Get professional advice before moving your retirement assets when you leave your job. Different approaches can cost or save you hundreds of thousands of dollars.

8. Select your financial advisor very carefully.

9. Consider the effect of income taxes, including state (and maybe local) taxes.

10. Look into making the maximum contributions to tax-deferred retirement plans where your employer matches at least part of your contribution (e.g., 401(k) plans—see Money-Smart Way #88).

PART ELEVEN
Money-Smart Ways
to Work

85. The best job for you

During your lifetime, you may have seven to 20 different jobs and possibly five to 10 careers. So what is the best first (or second or third) job for you?

Sit down and figure out what excites you. Then look for a job that includes your passion or may lead to a job that does. Think ahead so you don't waste years of your life.

The wrong jobs can ruin your health. The right ones can enhance your life as well as other lives around you.

Making a lot of money can help. But more important is controlling your spending and learning to save so you'll have the *financial independence to do the work you love* even if it does not pay as much as you'd like.

And remember this. You are not your work. What you do for work is part of you as a human being but it is not your entirety. Be the best you can be at whatever you choose to do.

Online job searching

Looking for a job isn't fun and it's time consuming. Below are some sites to make the process a bit easier. (For summer jobs, look at *www.Teens4Hire.org*, *www.CampJobs.com* and *www.SummerJobs.com*.)

America's Career Info Net is a one-step career and job center sponsored by the government. *www.acinet.org*

Indeed.com is a search engine for jobs that includes job listings from thousands of websites—major job boards, newspapers, associations and company career pages. Indeed, Inc., *www.indeed.com*

Jobster Search is a metasearch engine for jobs. Jobster, Inc., *www.jobster.com*

Monster is a well-known job search site. Monster Worldwide, Inc., *www.monster.com*

Simply Hired is a vertical search engine company whose goal is to build the largest online database of jobs on the planet. Simply Hired, Inc., *www.simplyhired.com*

Beware of online resume scams

Remember that a legitimate employer won't ask you to pay money to apply for a job or for promising you a job. The idea is that they pay you money, not the other way around.

Identity theft warning for job seekers

Be careful in posting resumes and responding to online job offers. Some identity thieves email "job application" and "background check" forms as a way to get your personal information.

Be cautious in posting information in online resumes

Along with being aware of false job postings, you should also be careful what information you put on your online resume.

The golden rule is to post only what you want an identity thief to see. The more generic, the better protected you will be. Think twice before posting a video resume.

Avoid posting your:

1. Social Security number

2. Drivers license number

3. Birth date

4. Birth place

5. Marital status

6. Street address

7. Current employer

8. Detailed work history

9. References

10. College name (it's easy for someone to contact a college and get your information from a college directory) and graduation date

For an online resume, have mail sent to a post office box rather than your home address and use a disposable email address that can be deleted when the job search is over.

Five important questions to ask before you post a resume

Ask the site (or find out the answers in the FAQs):

1. Will the resume be on there for a limited period of time?

2. Can a resume be deleted or revised by you?

3. Are resumes shared with other job sites? (This can affect whether you can delete your resume.)

4. Can personal information be kept anonymous?

5. What is the privacy policy for resumes and personal information?

Other considerations

A good site should have a privacy policy.

You might also want to go to the Better Business Bureau site (*www.bbb.org*) and read the employer's reliability report to make sure an employer is legitimate. Another site to check out is *www.lookstoogoodtobetrue.com*.

Contact an employer's human resources department to find out the company's proper hiring procedure and how you should submit your information. Human interaction is always the best policy. The more you can do face-to-face, the better chance you'll have to see if it's a real company that is worthwhile.

86. Part-time work

Working part-time can be valuable experience in many ways. Besides the money you earn, every position you take on is a learning experience. Use part-time work experiences to discover what work you'd like to do in the future and what you'll want to avoid. Find out what certain professions or jobs are like before you invest years of schooling in the field.

You can also use this work experience to learn about people and to see how they interact in the workplace, which may be very different from how they act in other situations.

Finally, part-time work can be an important part of your future resume or college/graduate school application showing the responsibilities you've taken on and the breadth of experience you're bringing with you.

87. Get it in writing

When you apply for a job, you usually have many interviews with a company. The topics of discussion include the type of work, your compensation, the benefits and your future with the company.

Finally, you may be offered a job. Usually, it's a verbal offer, not a written one.

There will probably come a time when you choose or are forced to leave the job. At that point, there may be misunderstandings (or worse) about what you were promised when you first accepted the job.

A way to minimize or avoid problems down the employment (or unemployment) road is to get your employer's promises and descriptions in writing before you start the job. If you're told it's unnecessary to put them in writing, think about what might happen if the person making the promises to you becomes disabled, dies, leaves the company or has a bad memory about that pre-employment discussion with you. You may have a difficult time confirming your understanding of the job requirements and benefits.

What you should have in hand before you start a job is:

- a detailed description of your job so there's no confusion about what is expected and the nature of the work you'll be doing
- the days and hours you'll be expected to work
- medical, vacation and retirement benefits
- compensation

The bottom line is to get it in writing *before* you start your job.

88. Job benefits

Before accepting a job, find out the benefits.

Retirement plans

Retirement plans come in many styles and flavors. The older type of retirement plan, a defined benefit plan, calls for the employer to make all the contributions. The now more-common 401(k) plan has employee contributions that may be matched in part, all or not at all by the employer.

Summary plan descriptions

Ask for a *Summary Plan Description* ("SPD") from your employer that tells you how retirement benefits are calculated and paid out. Read the description and ask questions until you really understand it.

There are three main things to look for in the SPD:

1. How much you can contribute to your retirement account

2. How much your employer will contribute

3. How soon or how long it will take for employer contributions and their earnings to belong to you (i.e., become "vested")

Your company retirement plan may be more important to you in the long run than Social Security benefits. Take the time to become educated. When you receive your employer's retirement plan statement each year, double-check it.

Before changing jobs and giving up your current retirement plan benefits, look at the new company's SPD to see what's in store for you.

401(k) plan tips

If you have a retirement plan at work, chances are it's a 401(k) plan. A 401(k) plans delays income tax until the retirement funds are withdrawn (i.e., it's a tax-deferred investment—see Money-Smart Way #81). This allows your nest egg to grow each year without income tax taking a bite during the growing years.

Five tips on your 401(k) plan

1. Don't say no to free money.

Although you, the employee, put in most of the contributions, usually your employer will match at least some of your contributions (up to certain limits).

If your company has one of those "matching" 401(k) plans and you're not participating at all or not participating to the fullest extent possible, you're giving up free money. Over the long haul, you could be passing up tens or hundreds of thousands of dollars including the growth of employer contributions.

2. Your 401(k) plan is not an ATM machine.

You may be able to borrow from your 401(k) for your short-term needs. But this is a retirement fund. If this isn't enough to convince you to resist temptation, remember that when you pay back your 401(k) loan, you're using after-tax money to do so and you may not receive an income tax deduction on the interest you're paying back. Also, if you leave your job and the plan requires repayment on the termination of employment, you may be taxed if the loan isn't repaid.

3. Leaving a job and dealing with your 401(k) can be complicated.

You may be able to leave the 401(k) money there, cash it in, transfer it to a new employer's 401(k) plan or roll it over to an IRA. Check with your company's 401(k) administrator before making a decision. In general, with any 401(k) or IRA withdrawal or transfer, try *not* to touch the money—it might trigger a taxable event. Instead, have the institutions work together to make a trustee-to-trustee transfer with you standing on the sidelines.

You may want to leave your retirement account in your former employer's retirement plan. Here's why. Boomerang employees are becoming more common. If you leave the company, withdraw your retirement account and later return to work for the same (or related) company, you may not receive credit under the retirement plan for your first work period. Take a look at the company's Summary Plan Description and obtain advice before making any decisions.

4. Avoid early withdrawals that incur penalties.

Although withdrawals are subject to income tax, there are times you may be able to avoid penalties. If you're not careful, early withdrawals could cause you to owe not only income tax on the withdrawn amount but also penalties.

5. 401(k) investments require your attention.

At least once a year, look at how your 401(k) investments are doing and whether they're meeting your long-term goals.

Health plans

Employee health benefits are changing every year. In the old days, employers paid all of the health insurance premiums. Now, the cost is usually shared by the employer and the employee with more and more of the cost shifted to the employee each year. The plans tend to cost more each year and to provide fewer or lower benefits.

If you're choosing between two comparable jobs, the one with a better health plan can be valuable to you. However, with job turnover so common and the likelihood that you'll be in good health in your younger years, what's most important is that you at least have a decent health plan in effect, even if it's not the best one. Uninsured medical bills can cause serious financial problems that can take years to resolve.

Other benefits

Your job may offer dental insurance, disability insurance, life insurance and other benefits. Depending on your personal and family circumstances, these could be important to you. Vacation and school-assistance benefits should be looked at, too.

For more on insurance, see Money-Smart Ways #93 through 96.

89. A few words about stock options

It's not uncommon to receive stock options from an employer as part of a compensation package. These options allow you to purchase shares in the company at a bargain price.

Stock options are sometimes used as a tradeoff for your taking a lower salary. Keep the following in mind as you ponder the value of these options.

First, you usually have to earn these options by working for the company for a period of time. For example, you may earn 25% of the options for each year of work, which means it would take four years for you to own all of your options.

Don't assume owning options is automatically a way to a fortune (although it might be). Options have value if the stock in the company is worth more than the bargain purchase price offered to you to exercise your option. Stocks go up and down in value. What was your bargain price to buy stock may turn out to be not that big a bargain.

Finally, you may lose your job before you've earned all or any part of your options.

90. How to develop the saving habit

Saving is a habit. Once you start saving, you'll be hooked for life. The best way to save is to have automatic withdrawals from every paycheck go directly into a savings or retirement account.

A one-year savings plan

Once you've got your debt under control (see Part Four), it's time to take the first saving step. Aim low and try to save 1% of your income in the first month. If you earn $2,000 per month, try to save $20 (the piggy bank technique in Money-Smart Way #65 should make this easy to do).

The next month, try to save 2% of your income ($40 in this example). For the next three months, increase your percentage by 1% per month (3% or $60, in the third month, 4% or $80 in the fourth month and 5% or $100 in the fifth month with this $2,000 salary per month example). If you miss your goal one month, try to reach it the next month. Try to keep up the 5% per month saving schedule for the next seven months to complete the year.

Don't get discouraged if you can't save 5% every month. Remember, if you miss your goal one month, try to reach it the next month.

Note that if you have to make a choice between paying off credit card debt or putting money into savings, it's *usually* better to pay off your credit card debt first (one exception might be a 401(k) plan with good employer matching contributions — see Money-Smart Way #88).

The year-two savings plan

You can stay at this 5% level for a couple of years or if you're really serious about protecting your future, read on for year two.

If all goes well, then in year two, try to save 1% more each month for the first five months (6% the first month, 7% the second month, 8% the third month, 9% the fourth month and 10% the fifth month). Then, stay at the 10% level for the next few years unless you can put even more away.

Again, if you can't reach the 10% goal, do the best you can. The idea is to develop the saving habit and maximize your savings while you're young. That way, compound growth will do a lot of the work for you over time to build your golden nest egg.

91. Preventing Social InSecurity

Once you start working, you should be concerned about Social Security.

When you think of Social Security, you usually just think of retirement benefits. But Social Security may also provide an additional package of benefits to you, a spouse and children long before retirement if you become severely disabled. Survivors' benefits may be paid, too, after your death. All of these benefits could amount to hundreds of thousands of dollars.

To avoid being shortchanged, you need to make sure Social Security has recorded your earnings correctly because it is your earnings that determine the benefit amounts for you and certain family members.

When you or your family members apply for any of these possible Social Security benefits, how will you or they know if the benefits are based on the correct amount of your earnings? There is a simple way to find out.

Form SSA-7004

To keep an eye on the information being used by Social Security, you need to complete a *Request for Social Security Statement* (Form SSA-7004). Once you're age 25 or older, you should automatically receive an annual earnings and benefit estimate statement.

The form is free and it's easy to obtain—log on to *www.ssa.gov* or call 800/772-1213 to order the form. Then just fill out the simple form and send it to the Social Security Administration.

Social Security will mail a listing of your earnings (according to their records) and a projection of your Social Security retirement, disability and survivor benefits. You just need to compare your earnings records with the benefit statement to determine whether the Social Security records are accurate. If there is any mistake in their records, you should have it corrected right away.

Here are two examples of mistakes that could have significant consequences. A digit may be left off (changing $31,000 to $3,100) or digits may be reversed (changing $31,000 to $13,000).

The name is the game

To avoid confusion in your Social Security records, always fill in your payroll forms exactly the same way. Don't sometimes use a full middle name and other times just an initial. Your best bet is to always use the exact name on your Social Security card as on your employment forms, including W-2 forms.

And for women who change their names upon marriage or divorce, make sure you advise Social Security of all name changes.

The time to check your Social Security records is long before benefits are to be claimed. In the year 2057 you probably won't be able to find your tax returns to verify your earnings in 2012. It's your responsibility to make sure Social Security lists your earnings correctly. Pay some attention to Social Security now so you don't lose out in the future.

92. Becoming an entrepreneur

It can be a great thrill and accomplishment to own your own business. It can also be one of the scariest and most financially dangerous steps you can take. Eight out of every ten businesses fail.

Not everyone is cut out to be an entrepreneur. Successful entrepreneurs have a special kind of personality that includes self-reliance, an ability to make decisions quickly and a belief in themselves and their business.

Before you plunk down your money (or your relatives' money) or borrow elsewhere to start a business, do yourself a favor and go to your local library to get the softcover or e-book edition of *Fail-Proof Your Business: Beat the Odds and Be Successful* by Paul E. Adams. As a successful entrepreneur who had several businesses, including one on the brink of disaster that he brought back to success, Adams shares in his book what can go wrong (and how to prevent it) with a small business and also the inside secrets of business success.

PART TWELVE
Money-Smart Ideas
for the Future

93. An apple a day and health insurance

Take good care of yourself. You may think you're indestructible now but how will you be at age 40 or 50 if you live your life carelessly or even recklessly? Pay attention to diet and exercise and chances are, you'll live a lot longer than that.

Health is more important than money for the quality of your life.

And part of taking care of your health is having health insurance. If you wait until you're sick to apply for insurance, you may not be able to get insurance at all or your illness/disease/condition may be excluded (or not covered until a lengthy waiting period goes by).

94. Disability insurance

Disability insurance provides you with an income when you're too disabled to work. Even if you have a disability policy through work, you may want to have one outside of work. Why? If you lose your job, you may lose your disability insurance, too.

Disability policies are not all the same. They can vary widely in cost and benefits. In general, there are two benefits from purchasing a policy while you are younger: (1) the cost is lower and (2) you are still insurable and not subject to a health condition that may disqualify you from coverage.

95. Life insurance

You may not need life insurance for quite a while. You may never need life insurance but you probably will. When you die, life insurance provides money to *beneficiaries* (people you name to receive the money).

Among the events that may cause a need for life insurance are buying a home, getting married, having children or owning a business.

Three key questions to ask before you buy

Before you buy life insurance, always ask yourself and your life insurance agent these three questions:

1. Why do I need this insurance?

2. What is the most this policy will cost me and for how many years under a worst-case scenario?

3. How much will I lose if I decide to cancel the policy early?

Buying the right amount and kind of life insurance

Analyze your purpose in buying a policy to determine the right amount and type of life insurance you need. The amount of insurance depends on why you are buying the insurance (e.g., to insure a good standard of living for your loved ones).

There are two main types of life insurance: *cash value* (which includes "whole life insurance") and *term*. There are variations of each type of policy. Term insurance has become more popular over time because, in general, you can get a larger death benefit for less money and be able to invest the premium difference in stocks, bonds, mutual funds and other investments. That's not to say that term insurance is always the right life insurance for you to select. However, a good starting point is to assume that you're going to purchase 20-year level-term insurance (see below) unless you can see why a different term period or cash value insurance would be a better choice for you.

Term insurance

Term insurance is the easier one to understand. Term insurance is like renting insurance — as long as you pay your premium, a death benefit will be paid upon your death. You don't own anything with term insurance. If you stop paying the premium, you generally walk away with nothing and no death benefit is payable. The term policies that do return your premiums are usually much more costly.

Term insurance is more often used to meet needs for specified time periods (e.g., for the next 20 years until I expect my toddler to graduate from college). Term insurance premium costs are lower at the beginning than cash value life insurance but they *may* increase rapidly as one gets older (since the risk of dying increases over time, too). However, some term insurance policies (*level-term policies*) can keep the premium at the same amount for the duration of the policy (e.g., for 10 or 20 years). One big risk with level-term insurance is that after a policy's level-rate period ends, you may not be able to afford the higher premiums under that policy for future years' coverage or be able to qualify for a new, substitute lower-cost policy due to health problems that occurred after you took out the first policy.

Cash value (and whole life) insurance

Cash value life insurance combines term insurance (it provides a death benefit) with a tax-deferred investment. A common type of cash value life insurance is whole life insurance. There are many types of cash value insurance.

Cash value life insurance generally costs more than term insurance during the earlier years but it is usually intended to provide lifelong insurance (rather than for just a specified period of time).

Get a sound company

As with any insurance, make sure the insurance company is rated highly by A.M. Best (*www.ambest.com*), Moody's (*www.moodys.com*), Standard & Poor's (*www.standardandpoors.com*), Weiss Research (*www.weissratings.com*) and Duff & Phelps (*www.duffandphelps.com*).

Get the ratings from your life insurance agent, the Net or your local library. Since life insurance is a long-term investment, you'll want to have your policy with a well-established and financially sound company that will still be around when the time comes to collect proceeds.

96. Naming life insurance and retirement plan beneficiaries

Here are two key tips in naming *beneficiaries* (one or more persons who will receive the financial "benefits" upon your death):

1. Name primary and backup ("contingent" or "secondary") beneficiaries in case your first choice does not survive you.

2. Keep your beneficiary designations up to date if circumstances change (e.g., if you break up with your boyfriend, you probably don't want him as your beneficiary).

97. Buying a home

To buy or not to buy, that is the question.

There are financial and psychological benefits with owning a home. Buying, rather than renting, *may* result in owning a substantial asset (especially once the loan has been paid off). When you make home loan (mortgage) payments, you are doing a form of saving. And the interest portion of mortgage payments may be deductible from your income tax (reducing your income tax bill). There are also special rules on selling a home that *may* make most or all of the gain income tax free.

On the other hand, homes can go down in value, even below what you owe on the property. You can lose your entire investment.

There are no absolute rules when it comes to real estate. In general, if you think you've settled down and you're going to own your home for at least five years, then consider buying a home. However, if your work situation is not stable enough to know that you'll live in the same area, think twice about the selling costs you'll need to pay and what will happen if you can't sell your home when you need to move. Renting, instead of owning, can be a wise move in many cases and give you more flexibility (including your choice of work in another part of the country or world).

How reliable you've been in paying your other bills can affect your home loan. If you're considered a good credit risk, you'll have a much easier time qualifying for a mortgage. You may be able to get "pre-approved" for a loan so you'll know the maximum amount you can afford to pay for a home. If you're seen as a poor credit risk, you either won't qualify for a loan or will often have to accept a loan with a higher rate of interest. See Money-Smart Way #31 on credit reports and credit scores.

98. How to take years off your home payments

There are many different types of loans with different interest rates, repayment amounts and loan repayment time periods. Generally, when you buy a home, your loan (the mortgage) usually takes 30 years to be paid off. If you buy your first house at 30, you'll still be making mortgage payments until age 60.

There are two ways to shorten the 30 years of mortgage payments. A longer life for a loan means your total interest payments over the loan will be higher. One way to shorten your loan payback is to take out a 15-year loan at the beginning instead of a 30-year loan. With a 15-year loan, the monthly payments are higher but the interest rate is lower. (The payments are higher — but not twice as high — even though you are paying off the loan twice as fast.)

Another way to pay your loan off faster and save interest is to have a 30-year loan and make extra voluntary payments in an amount you determine. A small but regular extra payment can result in your saving interest payments equal to 50% or more of the original loan amount.

99. Wills and trusts

Sooner or later, either you will need to have a will and/or a trust or you will be affected by one. It doesn't hurt to start learning about them now.

A *will* is a legal document that goes into effect after a person passes away and tells who will inherit the person's assets, who will manage the assets and who will take care of the person's minor children.

A *trust* is a similar document dealing just with assets. Some trusts are effective when the creator of the trust is alive and some come into play after a death.

Wills may need to go through a court process (probate) upon a death. Many trusts, such as a *living trust*, may avoid the court process.

If a person doesn't sign a will or trust, the state writes a will for the deceased person. The state says who will inherit assets, who will raise the children and when children will get total control of their share of any inheritance. The state's will also usually produces the worst tax results and higher legal and court-related costs.

100. Simplify your life

Simplification is becoming a major trend.

One way to deal with a shortage of time and money while improving your lifestyle is to simplify it.

By reducing your material needs, you gain freedom to make career changes and life decisions without being shackled by a financial ball and chain.

Four steps to reduce paperwork and get financial control

1. Consider automatic payouts for mortgage payments and health insurance premiums as well as automatic deductions from your paycheck or checking account for investments, retirement and college savings.

2. Have your paychecks automatically deposited.

3. Limit and consolidate the number of investments, mutual funds and retirement plans to a manageable number so your assets are diversified, but not too many in number. Too many small investments can lead to chaos and cause you to give up on trying to monitor what's happening where.

4. Limit yourself to one credit card (two at most) and pay off the outstanding balance every month.

101. Seven real-life money-smart skills

Congratulations! After finishing this book, you should now know how to:

1. Think about and save money

2. Make a budget and pay bills on time

3. Be a savvy shopper

4. Open and balance a checking account

5. Find and use the right credit card

6. Deal with college costs

7. Begin investing

Appendix

Brain teasers

Here are some brain teasers to solve yourself or to quiz your parents on (the answers start on page 151):

1. What are the earliest coins that have been found and what was unique about them?

2. What's the earliest paper money and what was it made from?

3. Who's the father of paper money in the United States?

4. Who came up with the ideas of "cents" and "dimes"?

5. When were credit cards first used?

6. When did ATMs start appearing?

7. What's been the biggest money around?

8. Where does the word "money" come from?

9. Where does the word "salary" come from?

10. Where does the word "bank" come from?

11. Why were checks a big change in banking?

12. How far back can we trace inflation (i.e., the cost of living going up over time)?

13. Where does the word "dollar" come from?

14. If inflation (the cost of living) goes up 6% per year, how long will it take for a $12 movie to cost $24?

15. If you get 10% interest on your money, how long will it take for your money to double?

16. Assume Sally. age 20, puts $2,000 per year into a retirement plan for 3 years and then stops making any contributions. Assume Joe, age 40, puts $2,000 per year into a similar plan for 20 years. If both retirement plans grow at 10% per year, who will have more money at age 60?

Answers to Brain Teasers

1. It depends upon your definition of coins. Around 600 B.C., the first coins were made from electrum. Electrum is a combination of gold and silver that occurs naturally. These coins were made in Lydia (now part of Turkey). The coins were made into the same size and weight and this turned out to be a big time-saver in commerce. Until then, silver and gold had to be weighed each time a trade or transaction was made. With standard coins, all that was necessary was to count the coins to complete a trade.

A thousand years earlier, China had its own form of coins – knife money and bronze spade money. Knives and spades were considered coins because they were virtually identical, had a guaranteed value and were deemed official by the state.

2. China was the first to use paper money around the year 1000. It was made from the bark of mulberry trees. Leaves from these trees, you may recall, are fed to caterpillars to produce silk. Marco Polo later wrote about this unique form of money.

3. Ben Franklin. He's on the $100 bill.

4. Thomas Jefferson. It was his idea to use the decimal system with "cent" from the Latin word for hundred and "dime" from the Latin for tenth.

5. The 1950s.

6. The 1970s.

7. In Yap (part of Micronesia in the Pacific), they've used stone money. Some of the stone disks have been up to 13 feet across. Although stone money may not be handy to use for shopping, it's sure hard to steal.

8. The Romans made a new silver coin, the denarius, in the temple of Juno Moneta. From Moneta, we have the word "money."

9. "Salary" comes from the Latin word "sal" meaning "of salt." Salt was a form of money from China to the Mediterranean. Besides its value in preserving and flavoring food, its pureness allowed it to be cut into standardized sizes to be used for purposes ranging from paying soldiers to trading for food.

10. Back in the 1300s, Italian banks were established. The word "bank" comes from the word "bench." Bankers transacted their business sitting on benches.

11. Until checks were invented by the Medici Bank in Florence, Italy, the only way to withdraw money from a bank was to appear in person and ask for a withdrawal.

12. Roman emperors needed to deal with inflation when paying their soldiers. Back in 46 B.C., soldiers received around 225 denarii under Julius Caesar's reign. Two hundred years or so later, Septimus Severus had to pay 600 denarii in 200 A.D. Twenty years later, inflation really took off and Maximinus paid 1,800 denarii.

13. Back in the early 1500s, in Bohemia (part of Germany), a new coin known as the thaler appeared. Soon any large silver coin was called a thaler. Over time, a thaler was called a dollar in England.

14. 12 years. Use the Rule of 72. Divide 72 by 6 (the 6% inflation rate) and the result is 12. In this case, the rule tells you how long it will take for prices to double rather than the size of your investments. For more information, see Money-Smart Way #68.

15. At 10% growth per year, it will take 7.2 years for your money to double. You use the Rule of 72 again to get this answer. Divide 72 by

the number (10) representing the yearly growth rate (10%) and the answer is 7.2 years. For more information, see Money-Smart Way #68.

16. Sally will. Through compound growth (letting her money work for her for a longer period of time), she'll have around $225,000 and Joe will have around $114,000. With just three contributions at an earlier age, Sally will have almost twice as much as Joe. Imagine how much she'd have if she continued to make the contributions. For more information, see Money-Smart Way #69.

Index

Life insurance (*cont.*)
cash value, 143-144
need for, 142-144
questions to ask on, 142
soundness of companies
and, 144
term, 143-144
types, 143-144
whole, 143-144
Lifetime Learning Tax Credits
83
Links, 16
Living trusts
avoiding probate and, 147
Loans. *See also* Mortgage.
college, 73-75, 77-79, 83, 84
401(k), 133-134
home, 7, 49, 145, 146
parents and, 61-63

M
Money market accounts, 85, 98
Money. *See also* Allowances,
Saving
definition of, 1-2
grades and, 64-65
mistakes with, 4-5
spending, 21-46
time and, 7-8
value of, 3-4
working and, 10
Mortgages, 7, 49, 83, 84, 124,
145, 146
MP3, 38

Mutual funds,
diversify, 110-111
income tax and, 119-120
information on, 118-120

N
Needs, 6-7
Net. *See* Internet; Websites.

O
Online banking, 85, 90, 96-97

P
Paperwork, 101-104
organizing, 104
receipts, 102-103
warranties and, 44-45
Parents
agreements with, 61-66
allowances and, 63-64
money agreements with,
61-63
siblings and, 65-66
Part-time work. *See* Work.
Passwords, 15-16
Peer pressure, 8, 9
Pension plan. *See* Retirement
plans
Price comparison,
Internet sites, 41-43
Prioritizing
expenditures, 22-24
goals and, 5, 7-8, 11-12, 98,

Time
  money and, 7-8
  TV and, 19
Tipping, 27
Traditional IRA. *See* IRA.
TransUnion, 48, 49
Trusts, 146-147
TV
  commercials and, 19-21
  shopping and, 20-21
  time and, 19

U
UGMA, 79
Uniform Gifts to Minors Act.
  See UGMA.
Uniform Transfers to Minors
  Act. *See* UTMA.
U.S. Savings Bonds, 82, 120-121
UTMA, 79

V
Value
  shopping for, 40
Voluntary simplicity, 9-11,
  147-148
Volunteering, 58-59

W
Wall Street Journal, 19
Wants, 6-7
Warranties, 44-45

Websites, 42, 43, 48, 49, 53, 59,

70, 72, 74, 75, 76, 80, 84, 128,
  130, 138, 144
Whole life insurance, 143-144
Wills, 146-147
Wireless networks, 18
Work
  benefits at, 132-135
  finding the right, 127-132
  401(k) and, 133-134
  online resumes and, 129-130
  online scams and, 128-129
  part-time, 130-131
  retirement benefits and,
    132-134
  saving at, 133-134
  searching for, 128
  security with, 69
  social networking sites and,
    13-14, 129
  stock options and, 135-136
  written agreements and,
    131-132

Book Description of

Organized to Be Your Best!
Transforming How You Work
5th Edition

by

Susan Silver

With over 250,000 in print for the first four editions, the fifth edition is the one book you need to get control over your desk, your computer and your demanding work life. You'll see how to:

☐ Control multiple, ever-changing projects and priorities, 24x7 work schedules and information overload

☐ Manage email, instant and text messages, phone calls and other communications

☐ Devise a time and information system just for you

☐ Work more collaboratively with others in person and online

☐ Master a messy desk as you learn to turn piles into files

☐ Maximize all your workspaces wherever they're located

☐ Get the most from your computer and mobile devices and protect yourself in the process

Susan Silver is the recognized organizing expert and bestselling author of the award-winning bible of organization *Organized to Be Your Best!* and the coauthor of *Teach Your Computer to Dance.*

Ms. Silver is a knowledgeable, entertaining and hands-on training and coaching professional who heads the company Positively Organized!

www.adams-hall.com

Book Description of

Teach Your Computer to Dance

by

Don Silver and Susan Silver

Life is getting more complex and so is technology. Whether it's your computer, a mobile device or the Internet, you need to know the right steps to control technology.

So take the lead and make technology dance to your tune. Loaded with the best tips and the latest advice on products, programs and websites, this book will show you how to be more secure and:

- ☐ Protect yourself, your computer and your mobile devices—on and off the Internet

- ☐ Control communication overload—email, instant and text messaging as well as cellphone/VoIP calls

- ☐ Discover better ways to search the Web to get quality, not quantity

- ☐ Find your digital notes, info and files easily and organize your computer

- ☐ Make the most of remote and collaborative computing

- ☐ Choose and use the right computer and mobile devices

"Great book for the computer genius or novice."
—Rochelle Stewart, Reporter and *Online Living* blogger, **The Boston Herald**

"You can pick any page at random and find yourself saying, 'That's a good idea.'"
—Andrew Kantor, Technology Columnist, **USA TODAY**

www.adams-hall.com